ANIMAL ENCYCLOPEDIAS

THE AFRICAN ANIMAL ENCYCLOPEDIA

BY BRENDA SCOTT ROYCE

Encyclopedias

An Imprint of Abdo Reference

abdobooks.com

TABLE OF CONTENTS

WELCOME TO AFRICA

Covering more than 11.7 million square miles (30.3 million sq km), Africa is Earth's second largest continent. It is surrounded by water on all sides. It lies between the Atlantic and Indian Oceans and the Mediterranean and Red Seas.

Several islands off the coast of Africa are considered to be part of the continent. Most notable among these is Madagascar. One of the world's largest islands, Madagascar is also one of the most biodiverse places on Earth.

Hippos are one of the most aggressive animals on Earth.

An elephant roams on the savanna in Namibia, Africa, during sunset.

CONSERVATION STATUS

The experts at the International Union for Conservation of Nature (IUCN) study animal species globally and categorize them based on their risk of extinction (on a scale from "critically endangered" to "least concern").

A conservation status of "least concern" doesn't mean that people are unconcerned about the species' survival. These species have a lower risk of extinction, though some may be declining. Every species is important in terms of global biodiversity.

The equator passes through the center of Africa. Most of the continent falls within the tropics, the regions between the Tropic of Cancer and the Tropic of Capricorn. As a result, the climate across the majority of the continent is hot and humid year-round. Highlands and coastal regions tend to be cooler.

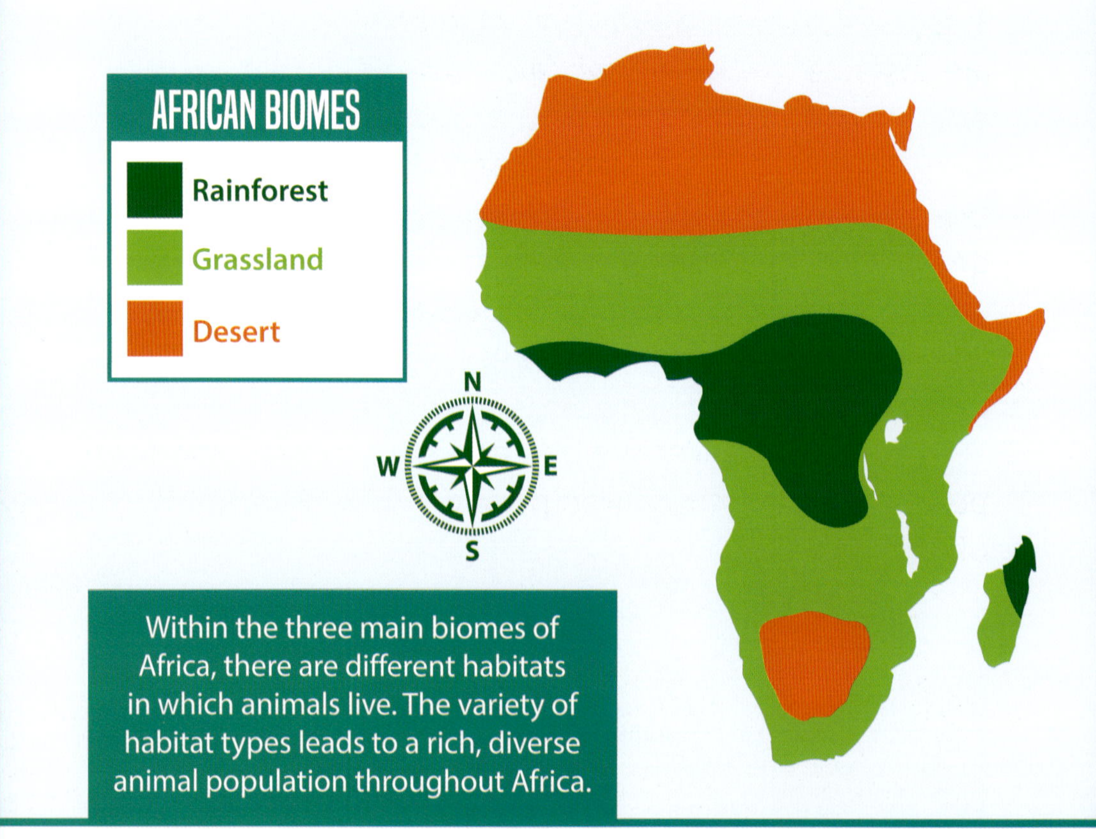

Africa has eight major habitat types. The central part of the continent is dominated by rainforests, which are filled with trees and an abundance of plant and animal life.

Woodlands are found in drier regions. These are sparsely covered with trees.

Grasslands are widespread across Africa. A savanna is a type of grassland with scattered trees and shrubs.

Africa is home to some of the world's largest deserts. The Sahara stretches across most of the northern continent.

The Kalahari covers a large part of southern Africa. Deserts are characterized by low rainfall, sparse vegetation, and extreme temperatures.

Semi-deserts are dry areas that have more rainfall than true deserts. Although still sparsely vegetated, they support a greater variety of plant life.

Africa has fewer high mountain ranges than any other continent. The most mountainous regions are found in East Africa.

Wetlands are covered with water, either temporarily or permanently. Marshes, swamps, and mud flats are types of wetlands.

A cheetah walks in the desert in southern Africa.

MAMMALS

Africa is known for its broad biodiversity, or variety of life, especially when it comes to mammals. It has more species of large mammals than any other continent.

Africa is home to some of the world's most recognizable species, such as lions, hippos, giraffes, and elephants. Other animals may seem strange, like the tenrec or the gundi. Mammals inhabit every habitat type in Africa. Many are endemic, meaning they are found nowhere else on Earth.

FUN FACT

Humans are mammals too.

Female and male lions roam the African savannas.

WHAT IS A MAMMAL?

- Mammals are warm-blooded animals. Their body temperature doesn't change with the environment but remains relatively constant.
- Female mammals produce milk to feed their young.
- Mammals are vertebrates.
- They have hair or fur on their bodies.
- In nearly all mammal species, females give birth to live young.

Wildebeest stand up shortly after they are born.

An elephant calf nurses from its mother.

AFRICAN CLAWLESS OTTER

ALL ABOUT

Although most otters have webbed paws, African clawless otters have fingers on their front paws. Rough skin on their palms helps them hold slippery fish. Despite their name, these otters aren't totally clawless. The middle digits of their hind feet have small claws that are used for grooming.

- **Length:** 2.5 to 3 feet (0.8 to 0.9 m)
- **Weight:** 22 to 48.5 pounds (10 to 22 kg)
- **Lifespan:** 10 to 12 years
- **Conservation Status:** Near Threatened

HABITAT & DIET

Clawless otters split their time between water and land, inhabiting rivers, lakes, and swamps. Large molars help them crush crabs. They also eat fish and other small animals.

FAMILY & SOCIAL LIFE

These otters live alone or in small groups.

FUN FACT

Clawless otters mark their territory by pooping along the perimeter.

CAPE FUR SEAL

ALL ABOUT

The Cape fur seal is a large pinniped, a group of mammals that includes sea lions and walruses. Cape fur seals divide their time between land and sea. Although they are excellent swimmers, they are clumsy on land. A thick layer of blubber and a double coat keeps them warm.

- **Length:** 6.5 to 8 feet (2 to 2.4 m)
- **Weight:** 265 to 660 pounds (120.2 to 299.4 kg)
- **Lifespan:** 18 to 25 years
- **Conservation Status:** Least Concern

HABITAT & DIET

Cape fur seals inhabit rocky coastlines. Their diet includes fish, octopus, squid, and crabs.

FAMILY & SOCIAL LIFE

Cape fur seals live in colonies ranging in size from a few dozen to a few thousand individuals.

FUN FACT

Other seal species visit Africa's coasts, but the Cape fur seal is a year-round resident.

DUGONG

ALL ABOUT

The dugong is a large marine mammal with thick skin and a flexible, trunk-like snout. It must surface every few minutes for air, but it can hold its breath for up to eight minutes. Dugongs look a lot like manatees, but they are smaller. In addition, a dugong's tail is V-shaped, whereas a manatee's is rounded.

- **Length:** 8 to 13 feet (2.4 to 4 m)
- **Weight:** 500 to 925 pounds (226.8 to 420 kg)
- **Lifespan:** 60 to 70 years
- **Conservation Status:** Vulnerable (globally), Critically Endangered (East African population)

HABITAT & DIET

Dugongs graze on seagrass in warm coastal waters.

FAMILY & SOCIAL LIFE

Dugongs typically live in pairs but sometimes travel in large herds.

FUN FACT

An all-grass diet makes dugongs gassy, but gas helps these massive marine mammals float.

HEAVISIDE'S DOLPHIN

ALL ABOUT

One of the smallest dolphin species, the Heaviside's dolphin is often mistaken for its main predator, the orca. Both have cone-shaped heads and similar black-and-white coloring, but orcas are about four times bigger.

- **Length:** 5.5 to 6 feet (1.7 to 1.8 m)
- **Weight:** 130 to 160 pounds (59 to 72.6 kg)
- **Lifespan:** 20 to 23 years
- **Conservation Status:** Near Threatened

HABITAT & DIET

The Heaviside's dolphin is found in cool, shallow waters. It mostly eats fish, squid, and octopus. When hunting, these dolphins use very high-frequency clicks that cannot be heard by orcas.

DID YOU KNOW?

Dolphins are one of more than 1,000 animals that echolocate, or use sound to find food and navigate their environment.

FAMILY & SOCIAL LIFE

These dolphins live in small pods, usually consisting of three to four members.

BAT-EARED FOX

ALL ABOUT

The bat-eared fox gets its name for its oversized ears, which it uses to detect insects, especially termites and dung beetles, underground. When the fox hears activity, it quickly digs. The bat-eared fox has more teeth than most mammals. These small teeth are designed for grinding insects rather than tearing into flesh.

- **Length:** 18 to 32 inches (45.7 to 81.3 cm)
- **Weight:** 6 to 10 pounds (2.7 to 4.5 kg)
- **Lifespan:** 4 to 6 years
- **Conservation Status:** Least Concern

FUN FACT

One bat-eared fox can consume more than one million termites a year.

HABITAT & DIET

In addition to insects, this fox eats rodents, lizards, chicks, and eggs. It lives in savannas and open plains.

ETHIOPIAN WOLF

ALL ABOUT

The Ethiopian wolf is one of the world's rarest wolves. With its long legs and tawny coat, it resembles a coyote. Adults mostly hunt alone but will team up when going after larger prey.

- **Length:** 3 to 3.9 feet (0.9 to 1.2 m)
- **Weight:** 24 to 42 pounds (10.9 to 19.1 kg)
- **Lifespan:** 8 to 10 years
- **Conservation Status:** Endangered

HABITAT & DIET

This wolf only lives in the highlands of Ethiopia. Its diet consists almost entirely of rats and rodents. Wolves feed their pups by regurgitating food into their mouths.

FAMILY & SOCIAL LIFE

These wolves live in tight-knit packs of up to 13. Adults cooperatively care for and feed youngsters.

DID YOU KNOW?

Biologists are vaccinating Ethiopian wolves against diseases also found in domestic dogs. Medicine is hidden inside meat that is placed in a field for the wolves to find.

FENNEC FOX

ALL ABOUT

The fennec fox is the smallest wild dog species. Light coloring helps this desert dweller blend with its environment. Fur on the soles of its feet allows it to walk on hot sand. The fennec's large ears release body heat and help the fox find underground prey.

- **Length:** 17 to 28 inches (43.2 to 71.1 cm)
- **Weight:** 1.5 to 3.3 pounds (0.7 to 1.5 kg)
- **Lifespan:** 9 to 11 years
- **Conservation Status:** Least Concern

HABITAT & DIET

This fox inhabits dry deserts. Its varied diet includes rodents, lizards, insects, birds, and fruit.

FAMILY & SOCIAL LIFE

They live in small family groups of up to 10 foxes.

FUN FACT

They belong to the dog family, but fennec foxes can purr like a cat.

JACKAL

Black-backed jackal

ALL ABOUT

There are three types of jackals that inhabit Africa. The black-backed jackal has a triangle of black fur running along its back. The side-striped jackal has stripes on its sides. These medium-sized members of the canine family are closely related to wolves.

- **Length:** 3.3 to 4.5 feet (1 to 1.4 m)
- **Weight:** 17 to 25 pounds (7.7 to 11.3 kg)
- **Lifespan:** 8 to 9 years
- **Conservation Status:** Least Concern

FUN FACT

Other jackals howl, but the side-striped jackal hoots like an owl.

HABITAT & DIET

These carnivores will hunt live prey or scavenge the remains of another predator's kill. They occupy a wide range of habitats.

FAMILY & SOCIAL LIFE

Jackals live in small family groups but will gather in large packs to hunt. Males and females share parenting duties.

PAINTED DOG

ALL ABOUT

The painted dog's fur looks like it was painted with splotches of black, brown, yellow, and white. This coloring provides excellent camouflage when they hunt in tall grass.

- **Length:** 30 to 56 inches (76.2 to 142.2 cm)
- **Weight:** 40 to 70 pounds (18.1 to 31.8 kg)
- **Lifespan:** 10 to 12 years
- **Conservation Status:** Endangered

HABITAT & DIET

Painted dogs inhabit savannas and woodlands. These carnivores work as a team to hunt a variety of prey, including antelopes, warthogs, rabbits, and birds. One pack member will often distract or restrain prey while the others move in for the kill.

DID YOU KNOW?

Painted dogs have about an 80 percent success rate in taking down prey. This makes them more efficient hunters than either lions or cheetahs.

FUN FACT

Each painted dog's coat pattern is unique. This helps pack members recognize each other.

FAMILY & SOCIAL LIFE

Painted dogs live in large packs and are rarely aggressive with one another. Only the dominant pair produce offspring. The other adults cooperate to hunt, raise pups, and watch out for danger. They take care of family, sharing food with sick, injured, and elderly pack members.

AFRICAN BUSH ELEPHANT

ALL ABOUT

Scientists currently recognize three elephant species: the African bush elephant, the African forest elephant, and the Asian elephant, which is only found in Asia. The African bush elephant is also known as the savanna elephant. It is the biggest of the three elephant species and the largest land mammal on Earth.

All elephants have a long, flexible trunk that serves many functions. Not only used for breathing, this elongated nose is used as a trumpet, a hose, and a grasping tool. Both male and female African elephants have tusks made of ivory.

- **Length:** 10 to 13 feet (3 to 4 m)
- **Weight:** 9,900 to 14,000 pounds (4,490.6 to 6,350.3 kg)
- **Lifespan:** up to 70 years
- **Conservation Status:** Endangered

DID YOU KNOW?

Despite their massive size, elephants are afraid of bees. To keep elephants away from their crops, some farmers place beehives along their fences.

HABITAT & DIET

These herbivores live on the savanna, where they eat leaves, grasses, twigs, bark, and fruit.

FAMILY & SOCIAL LIFE

An elephant herd is made up of females and young. The oldest female is usually the leader.

Females stay with the herd for life, whereas males leave when they grow up. Adult males may form small bachelor groups or remain solitary.

FUN FACT

An elephant's tusks are its incisor teeth. They never stop growing.

AFRICAN FOREST ELEPHANT

ALL ABOUT

Forest elephants prefer to live in dense rainforests. Compared with bush elephants, their bodies are smaller and their tusks are straighter. They also have fewer toes. Bush elephants have five toes on their front feet and four on their back feet, whereas forest elephants have four in front and three in back.

- **Length:** 7 to 10 feet (2.1 to 3 m)
- **Weight:** 4,000 to 12,000 pounds (1,814.4 to 5,443.1 kg)
- **Lifespan:** up to 70 years
- **Conservation Status:** Critically Endangered

HABITAT & DIET

Fruit dominates the forest elephant's diet. It also eats plants, leaves, grass, and bark.

FAMILY & SOCIAL LIFE

Forest elephants live in small groups made up of females and their offspring. Males tend to be solitary.

FUN FACT

The forest elephant is the smallest elephant species.

DID YOU KNOW?

One of the elephant's relatives is the elephant shrew, which is only about 6 inches (15.2 cm) long.

Elephant shrew

BLACK-FOOTED CAT

ALL ABOUT

The black-footed cat is smaller than the average house cat. Its soft, thick coat is marked with spots and stripes. It has large eyes, a short tail, and low-set ears. This nocturnal hunter is shy but can be fierce if confronted.

- **Length:** 14 to 20 inches (35.6 to 50.8 cm)
- **Weight:** 2.2 to 5 pounds (1 to 2.3 kg)
- **Lifespan:** 8 to 10 years
- **Conservation Status:** Vulnerable

FUN FACT

This cat's habit of resting in termite mounds earned it the nickname "anthill tiger."

HABITAT & DIET

During the day, black-footed cats hide in unoccupied underground burrows made by springhares, squirrels, or other animals. They will also rest in hollow termite mounds. Rodents and birds are their primary prey.

FAMILY & SOCIAL LIFE

Other than females with kittens, these cats live alone.

CARACAL

ALL ABOUT

The caracal is a medium-sized feline with a yellowish or reddish coat and white underside. Its ear tips have long tufts. The function of these tufts is debated. They may enhance hearing or communication. A caracal has more than 20 muscles in each ear and can move them in many directions.

- **Length:** 27 to 43 inches (68.6 to 109.2 cm)
- **Weight:** 18 to 42 pounds (8.2 to 19.1 kg)
- **Lifespan:** about 12 years
- **Conservation Status:** Least Concern

HABITAT & DIET

The caracal lives in grasslands, forests, and desert scrublands. It hunts small mammals, birds, and reptiles.

FAMILY & SOCIAL LIFE

These cats lead solitary lives, coming together only to mate.

FUN FACT

A caracal can leap up to 10 feet (3 m) to snatch a bird in flight.

CHEETAH

ALL ABOUT

The cheetah has long legs, powerful muscles, and a flexible spine that enable it to run up to 70 miles per hour (112.7 kmh). Wide nostrils and enlarged lungs allow it to take in extra oxygen for the chase. Unlike other big cats, the cheetah hunts during the day.

- **Length:** 3.5 to 5 feet (1.1 to 1.5 m)
- **Weight:** 75 to 140 pounds (34 to 63.5 kg)
- **Lifespan:** up to 15 years
- **Conservation Status:** Vulnerable

HABITAT & DIET

Cheetahs inhabit deserts, grasslands, and plains. Their prey includes rabbits, antelopes, and other small animals.

FAMILY & SOCIAL LIFE

Cheetahs are solitary except when females care for cubs. Cubs have fluffy manes that disappear as they mature.

FUN FACT

Unlike most cats' claws, a cheetah's claws don't retract.

DID YOU KNOW?

Some farmers in Africa use guard dogs to protect their cows from cheetah attacks. The dogs chase away predators.

LEOPARD

ALL ABOUT

Leopards are the smallest of the big cats, a group that also includes lions, tigers, jaguars, and snow leopards. The shade of a leopard's coat varies based on its habitat, with grassland populations being lighter than forest dwellers. These ambush predators are excellent climbers. They will carry prey into a tree to avoid it being snatched by scavengers. After a night spent hunting, they can be seen dozing on high branches.

- **Length:** 5 to 7.5 feet (1.5 to 2.3 m)
- **Weight:** 46 to 165 pounds (20.9 to 74.8 kg)
- **Lifespan:** 12 to 15 years
- **Conservation Status:** Vulnerable

DID YOU KNOW?

A leopard looks a lot like a jaguar, but the two are found on different continents. Both have spots called rosettes. A jaguar's rosettes have spots inside them, whereas a leopard's do not.

HABITAT & DIET

Leopards inhabit forests and grasslands. Their prey ranges in size from rodents to antelopes.

FAMILY & SOCIAL LIFE

Cubs spend up to two years with their mother. Otherwise, the species is solitary.

FUN FACT

Different populations have differently shaped spots. The spots are circular in eastern Africa and squarish in the south.

FUN FACT

A lion's roar can be heard from 5 miles (8 km) away.

LION

ALL ABOUT

The lion is an apex predator, the top of its food chain. Females are significantly smaller than males, and they lack manes. Dominant males have the darkest manes. A thick, heavy mane also protects the male's head and neck in battle.

- **Length:** 5 to 10 feet (1.5 to 3 m)
- **Weight:** 270 to 570 pounds (122.5 to 258.5 kg)
- **Lifespan:** 14 to 18 years
- **Conservation Status:** Vulnerable

DID YOU KNOW?

A male's main job is to protect the pride while female lions do most of the hunting. But males eat first and control who gets which parts of the carcass.

HABITAT & DIET

These big cats are commonly seen on the savanna, but they also occupy deserts and woodlands. They hunt at night, primarily preying upon large hoofed mammals such as antelopes, zebra, and wildebeest.

FAMILY & SOCIAL LIFE

Lions live in large family groups called prides. An average pride contains up to three males, a dozen females, and their young.

SAND CAT

ALL ABOUT

Pale sandy fur helps the sand cat blend into desert landscapes. Sand cats spend their days in underground burrows to avoid the heat, emerging at night to hunt. They meow but will also make loud barking sounds.

- **Length:** 18 to 22 inches (45.7 to 55.9 cm)
- **Weight:** 3 to 7.5 pounds (1.4 to 3.4 kg)
- **Lifespan:** 7 to 10 years
- **Conservation Status:** Least Concern

HABITAT & DIET

The sand cat lives only in deserts. It seldom drinks water, getting all the moisture it needs from its prey, which includes reptiles, birds, rabbits, and insects.

FAMILY & SOCIAL LIFE

Sand cats are solitary. Kittens grow up fast, becoming independent at about four months old.

FUN FACT

Thick fur on their soles lets sand cats walk across sand without leaving footprints.

SERVAL

ALL ABOUT

The serval is a medium-sized cat with long legs and a long neck. Large, upright ears can rotate independently to pinpoint the sound of prey. Servals can even hear the ultrasonic sounds produced by rodents underground.

- **Length:** 2 to 3.3 feet (0.6 to 1 m)
- **Weight:** 18 to 40 pounds (8.2 to 18.1 kg)
- **Lifespan:** about 10 years
- **Conservation Status:** Least Concern

HABITAT & DIET

Servals live in grasslands, woodlands, and wetlands. They prey upon rodents, frogs, birds, and other small animals.

FAMILY & SOCIAL LIFE

Except when they are finding mates or raising young, these cats lead solitary lives.

DID YOU KNOW?

White spots on the back of a serval's ears are thought to help youngsters follow their mother through grass. Tigers have similar spots on their ears.

ADDAX

ALL ABOUT

The addax is a grayish-white antelope with long, spiral horns and a chestnut-colored tuft of hair on its forehead. Highly mobile, the addax will travel great distances in search of vegetation. In extreme heat, they will dig shallow depressions in the sand to rest in.

- **Length:** 5 to 5.5 feet (1.5 to 1.7 m)
- **Weight:** 130 to 280 pounds (59 to 127 kg)
- **Lifespan:** up to 19 years
- **Conservation Status:** Critically Endangered

HABITAT & DIET

These herbivores graze on grasses and plants in the Sahara Desert. They also eat fruit and seed pods.

FUN FACT

An addax's horns can reach 3.5 feet (1.1 m) in length.

FAMILY & SOCIAL LIFE

Addax live in small herds led by a dominant male.

AFRICAN WILD DONKEY

ALL ABOUT

The African wild donkey is a member of the horse family. It has a grayish body, white belly, and zebra-like stripes on its legs. Its wide eyes are located on the sides of its head, giving it excellent peripheral vision.

- **Length:** 6.5 to 7.5 feet (2 to 2.3 m)
- **Weight:** 500 to 600 pounds (226.8 to 272.2 kg)
- **Lifespan:** 25 to 40 years
- **Conservation Status:** Critically Endangered

FUN FACT

This animal is believed to be the ancestor of modern-day domestic donkeys.

HABITAT & DIET

The African wild donkey eats grasses and plants, including thorny types. It inhabits rocky deserts and semiarid bushlands.

FAMILY & SOCIAL LIFE

Wild donkeys don't live in stable groups. They come together in small, temporary herds.

BARBARY SHEEP

ALL ABOUT

The Barbary sheep is more closely related to a goat than to sheep. Long hair flowing down its chest may be its most distinctive feature. Its thick horns curve outward and are present on both males and females.

- **Length:** 4.24 to 5.5 feet (1.3 to 1.7 m)
- **Weight:** 88 to 320 pounds (39.9 to 145.1 kg)
- **Lifespan:** about 10 years
- **Conservation Status:** Vulnerable

HABITAT & DIET

These wild sheep live in mountains and deserts. They eat a variety of plant matter.

FAMILY & SOCIAL LIFE

They most often live in mixed herds of males, females, and offspring.

BONGO

ALL ABOUT

The bongo is a colorful, large-bodied antelope with spiral horns. Its chestnut-red coat has vertical white stripes. Other white markings include spots on its face and chest and bands on its legs. The bongo tilts its head back when running to avoid getting its horns tangled in vines and branches.

- **Length:** 5.5 to 8.3 feet (1.7 to 2.5 m)
- **Weight:** 460 to 890 pounds (208.7 to 403.7 kg)
- **Lifespan:** 20 to 25 years
- **Conservation Status:** Critically Endangered (mountain)

HABITAT & DIET

Bongos are found in both lowland and mountain forests. Their diet includes grasses, leaves, and roots.

FAMILY & SOCIAL LIFE

Male bongos are solitary. Females live in small- to medium-sized herds.

CAPE BUFFALO

ALL ABOUT

The Cape buffalo is the largest and most common of the four African buffalo subspecies. It has a thick hide and nearly black coat. Both genders have curved horns, but males' horns are much bigger and can reach more than 5 feet (1.5 m) long. Cape buffalo are known for their ornery temper. They will stand up to a lion rather than run away.

- **Length:** 7 to 11 feet (2.1 to 3.4 m)
- **Weight:** 600 to 1,900 pounds (272.2 to 861.8 kg)
- **Lifespan:** 11 to 22 years
- **Conservation Status:** Near Threatened

HABITAT & DIET

Cape buffalo graze on plants and grasses. They are found near water sources in savannas, forests, and woodland habitats.

DID YOU KNOW?

A symbiotic relationship has evolved between buffalo and oxpeckers. Oxpeckers ride on buffalo, eating ticks and other insects from their bodies. The birds, in turn, warn the buffalo of approaching predators.

FAMILY & SOCIAL LIFE

Cape buffalo live in herds of up to a few thousand.

FUN FACT

When faced with a predator, the herd forms a protective circle around calves.

DROMEDARY CAMEL

ALL ABOUT

The dromedary camel has a single hump. Its cousin, the Bactrian camel (a native of Asia), has two. The hump stores fat, which can be burned for energy. These animals can tolerate extreme heat and go months without drinking water.

- **Height:** 6 to 7 feet (1.8 to 2.1 m)
- **Weight:** 660 to 1,500 pounds (299.4 to 680.4 kg)
- **Lifespan:** up to 40 years
- **Conservation Status:** Not Threatened

HABITAT & DIET

Dromedaries are desert dwellers who eat leaves, plants, and grasses.

FAMILY & SOCIAL LIFE

A herd usually consists of one male, multiple females, and their young.

DID YOU KNOW?

Now extinct in the wild, dromedaries were domesticated thousands of years ago for transportation, milk, and wool. Today, most live in free-ranging herds under human control.

DUIKER

Black duiker

ALL ABOUT

Duikers are small-bodied antelopes with arched backs and short, straight horns. About two dozen different species exist. Easily startled, they get their name from their habit of diving into thickets when frightened. *Duiker* means "to dive" in Afrikaans and Dutch.

- **Height:** 12 to 35 inches (30.5 to 89 cm)
- **Weight:** 7 to 180 pounds (3.2 to 81.6 kg)
- **Lifespan:** 5 to 12 years
- **Conservation Status:** Varies by species

HABITAT & DIET

Duikers inhabit dense forests. They primarily eat leaves and fruit, but they will consume small animals on occasion.

FAMILY & SOCIAL LIFE

Most duikers live alone or in pairs.

FUN FACT

The dark markings under a duiker's eyes are scent glands.

Common duiker

ELAND

ALL ABOUT

The eland is the world's largest antelope. There are two species: common and giant. Both are larger than any other antelope. Elands have spiral horns. The giant eland's horns grow up to 4 feet (1.2 m) long.

- **Length:** 6.7 to 9.5 feet (2 to 2.9 m)
- **Weight:** 660 to 2,200 pounds (299.4 to 997.9 kg)
- **Lifespan:** 15 to 25 years
- **Conservation Status:** Varies by species

FUN FACT

When eland walk, their tendons make sharp clicks. These clicks help them communicate their location.

HABITAT & DIET

They inhabit forests and grasslands. These herbivores primarily eat leaves, twigs, and flowers.

FAMILY & SOCIAL LIFE

Elands form herds of varying sizes, with older males often living alone or in bachelor herds.

GERENUK

ALL ABOUT

The gerenuk is a medium-sized antelope with an unusually long neck. Males have S-shaped horns. Standing upright on its hind legs, the gerenuk eats leaves off high branches and tall shrubs. This feeding posture allows gerenuk to reach foliage that other antelopes can't.

- **Length:** 4.6 to 5.3 feet (1.4 to 1.6 m)
- **Weight:** 63 to 128 pounds (28.6 to 58.1 kg)
- **Lifespan:** 10 to 12 years
- **Conservation Status:** Near Threatened

HABITAT & DIET

Gerenuks avoid open grassland, preferring semiarid brushland with places to hide. They eat acacia and other leaves.

FAMILY & SOCIAL LIFE

Males are solitary, whereas females form small herds. Gerenuk mothers hide their newborn calves while they forage.

FUN FACT

When standing on its hind legs to eat, a gerenuk can reach 6 feet (1.8 m) tall.

GIRAFFE

ALL ABOUT

The tallest animal on land, giraffes are the lookout towers of the African savanna. Their long necks not only allow them to keep watch for danger but also eat what other animals cannot reach. Several types of giraffes exist, each with its own spot pattern. The knobs on a giraffe's head are called ossicones. Unlike horns, they are covered with skin and hair.

- **Height:** up to 19 feet tall (5.8 m)
- **Weight:** 1,800 to 3,000 pounds (816.5 to 1,360.8 kg)
- **Lifespan:** up to 26 years
- **Conservation Status:** Vulnerable

DID YOU KNOW?

Giraffes spread their legs to drink because their necks are too short to reach the ground when standing straight.

HABITAT & DIET

Giraffes are primarily leaf eaters, with acacia leaves being their preferred food. Long, nimble tongues allow them to pick around acacia thorns. Most giraffes live in savannas and shrublands.

FAMILY & SOCIAL LIFE

A giraffe herd is called a tower and can include up to 20 females and young. Males may be solitary or form bachelor herds.

FUN FACT

Giraffes are mostly silent, but some hum while they sleep.

HIPPOPOTAMUS

ALL ABOUT

Hippopotamus comes from the Greek words for "river horse." True to its name, the hippo is equally at home on land and in the water. These massive mammals spend most of the day resting in the water. At night, they emerge to graze on land. Hippos have large, barrel-shaped bodies and short tails.

FUN FACT

A hippo can eat up to 130 pounds (59 kg) of grass in a single night.

Though their lifestyle revolves around water, hippos don't swim. They stand, walk, or bounce on the bottom and can remain submerged for several minutes.

- **Length:** 4.9 to 16.5 feet (1.5 to 5 m)
- **Weight:** 400 to 9,000 pounds (181.4 to 4,082.3 kg)
- **Lifespan:** up to 40 years
- **Conservation Status:** Varies by species

HABITAT & DIET

Hippos inhabit rivers, swamps, and lakes. Grass makes up the bulk of their diet. They will also eat some aquatic plants.

FAMILY & SOCIAL LIFE

Highly social, hippos live in small family pods but sometimes gather by the hundreds.

DID YOU KNOW?

The hippopotamus's cousin, the pygmy hippo, weighs about one-tenth as much as a common hippo. Pygmy hippos also have longer legs, smaller heads, and spend less time in the water.

IMPALA

ALL ABOUT

This antelope has a light brown coat and white belly. Males have spiral horns.

- **Length:** 3.5 to 5 feet (1.1 to 1.5 m)
- **Weight:** 99 to 132 pounds (44.9 to 59.9 kg)
- **Lifespan:** 13 to 15 years
- **Conservation Status:** Least Concern

FAMILY & SOCIAL LIFE

These fast runners live in large herds. A herd will scatter in all directions to confuse predators.

KLIPSPRINGER

ALL ABOUT

This antelope stands less than 2 feet (0.6 m) tall. It prefers rocky terrain and jumps very high.

- **Length:** 2.5 to 3.5 feet (0.8 to 1.1 m)
- **Weight:** 18 to 40 pounds (8.2 to 18.1 kg)
- **Lifespan:** up to 15 years
- **Conservation Status:** Least Concern

FAMILY & SOCIAL LIFE

Klipspringers live in pairs. They take turns eating and looking for danger.

KUDU

ALL ABOUT

The kudu is a large antelope known for its huge corkscrew horns, found only on males. Two species exist, greater and lesser, differentiated mainly by size.

- **Length:** 3.6 to 6.8 feet (1.1 to 2.1 m)
- **Weight:** 130 to 600 pounds (59 to 272.2 kg)
- **Lifespan:** 7 to 15 years
- **Conservation Status:** Varies by species

HABITAT & DIET

These shy antelope prefer forests and woodland habitats. They dine on leaves, vines, fruit, and flowers.

FUN FACT

The greater kudu has the largest horns of any antelope. They can be up to 6 feet (1.8 m) long.

FAMILY & SOCIAL LIFE

Kudu are peaceful animals that don't battle over territory. They live in small herds.

OKAPI

ALL ABOUT

Viewed from behind, the okapi has stripes like a zebra's, but its closest relative is the giraffe. Like giraffes, the okapi has two furry ossicones on its head. Its dark brown fur is thick and velvety. Its stripes help the okapi blend into dense forests.

- **Height:** about 5 feet (1.5 m)
- **Weight:** 440 to 770 pounds (199.6 to 349.3 kg)
- **Lifespan:** 20 to 30 years
- **Conservation Status:** Endangered

HABITAT & DIET

The okapi is only found in one country, the Democratic Republic of the Congo. It lives in dense rainforests and uses its long, prehensile tongue to pluck leaves from trees.

FAMILY & SOCIAL LIFE

Unlike giraffes, okapi don't form herds. Other than mothers with calves, they lead solitary lives.

FUN FACT

The okapi can use its long tongue to groom its ears and nose.

ORYX

Arabian oryx

ALL ABOUT

Oryx are large-bodied antelopes with long, ridged horns.

- **Length:** 5 to 6.2 feet (1.5 to 1.9 m)
- **Weight:** 140 to 524 pounds (63.5 to 237.7 kg)
- **Lifespan:** up to 20 years
- **Conservation Status:** Varies by species

HABITAT & DIET

These desert dwellers can go months without drinking water. They eat grasses, herbs, and plants.

RED RIVER HOG

ALL ABOUT

Red river hogs have reddish-orange hair and wispy ear tufts. Piglets have stripes.

- **Length:** 40 to 50 inches (101.6 to 127 cm)
- **Weight:** 100 to 265 pounds (45.4 to 120.2 kg)
- **Lifespan:** up to 20 years
- **Conservation Status:** Least Concern

HABITAT & DIET

Red river hogs live in rainforests and savannas. They eat roots, tubers, and fungi.

RHINOCEROS

ALL ABOUT

Two of the world's five rhinoceros species can be found in Africa: the white rhino and the black rhino. The white rhinoceros is the larger of the two. White rhinos also have a wide, squarish upper lip. Black rhinos have a pointed upper lip. Both species have two horns. Rhino horn is made of keratin, the same substance as human fingernails.

- **Length:** 10 to 14 feet (3 to 4.3 m)
- **Weight:** 1,750 to 6,600 pounds (793.8 to 2,993.7 kg)
- **Lifespan:** 30 to 50 years
- **Conservation Status:** Varies by species

Black rhino

FUN FACT

Black rhinos and white rhinos are shades of the same color, gray.

HABITAT & DIET

White rhinos live on savannas, where they graze primarily on grass. Black rhinos inhabit forests, scrublands, and savannas. They use their flexible upper lip to grasp leaves, twigs, and other plants.

White rhino

FAMILY & SOCIAL LIFE

The white rhino is the most social of all the rhino species. They may live in a small group, called a crash. Black rhinos are solitary, except for mothers and calves.

DID YOU KNOW?

All rhinos are in danger of extinction due to poaching for their horns. In South Africa, scent-detection dogs are helping to protect rhinos by tracking down poachers.

SPEKE'S GAZELLE

ALL ABOUT

The Speke's gazelle is a small antelope with folds of skin on its nose that can inflate to the size of a golf ball. This adaptation cools blood flowing to the gazelle's brain. It also produces a loud, honking sneeze to warn others of danger.

- **Length:** 3 to 3.5 feet (0.9 to 1.1 m)
- **Weight:** 25 to 40 pounds (11.3 to 18.1 kg)
- **Lifespan:** up to 12 years
- **Conservation Status:** Endangered

HABITAT & DIET

Speke's gazelles live in harsh desert and semi-desert habitats. They eat dry grasses and leaves.

FAMILY & SOCIAL LIFE

Gazelles form small- and medium-sized herds.

DID YOU KNOW?

The Speke's gazelle is part of the family that includes bison and other antelopes.

WARTHOG

ALL ABOUT

What seem like warts on a warthog are actually fatty bumps that protect the warthog's face during battle. Warthogs have two sets of tusks that they use to dig up food, fight off predators, and compete with one another. Like other swine, warthogs are fond of wallowing in mud, but in the dry season, they can go months without access to mud or water.

- **Length:** 3 to 5 feet (0.9 to 1.5 m)
- **Weight:** 110 to 330 pounds (49.9 to 149.7 kg)
- **Lifespan:** up to 15 years
- **Conservation Status:** Least Concern

FUN FACT

When a warthog opens its mouth, its lower tusks sharpen themselves against its upper tusks.

HABITAT & DIET

These omnivores eat whatever they can find. They inhabit grasslands and woodlands.

FAMILY & SOCIAL LIFE

Adult males are mostly solitary. Females and young form groups known as sounders.

WILDEBEEST

ALL ABOUT

The wildebeest is a member of the antelope family. There are two species: black and blue. Both possess large, curved horns and shaggy manes. The black wildebeest is dark brown to black. Blue wildebeest aren't actually blue. Their gray coat can appear to have a bluish or silvery tint.

Blue wildebeest are always on the move. Their annual trek, known as the Great Migration, takes them on a roughly 1,200-mile (1,931.2 km) circular route in search of fresh grass and water. An estimated two million wildebeest take part in the journey, accompanied by zebras, gazelles, and other animals.

- **Length:** 5.5 to 8 feet (1.7 to 2.4 m)
- **Weight:** 240 to 600 pounds (108.9 to 272.2 kg)
- **Lifespan:** up to 20 years
- **Conservation Status:** Least Concern

Blue wildebeest

Black wildebeest

HABITAT & DIET

Wildebeest inhabit savannas and woodlands. Most females give birth around the same time. Over a three-week birthing period, thousands of wildebeest calves are born each day.

FAMILY & SOCIAL LIFE

Wildebeest live in large herds. Herds of blue wildebeest can number in the millions. A black wildebeest herd is considerably smaller.

FUN FACT

A wildebeest is also known as a gnu.

Grevy's zebra

ZEBRA

ALL ABOUT

The zebra is a wild member of the horse family. There are three zebra species, identified by the width of their stripes. The Grevy's zebra has narrow stripes, the plains zebra has wide stripes, and the mountain zebra is in between. Zebras have short, stiff manes. Large ears and wide-set eyes help zebras detect predators from far away.

FUN FACT

A zebra foal can stand and walk within minutes of birth.

- **Length:** 6.9 to 9.0 feet (2.1 to 2.8 m)
- **Weight:** 450 to 990 pounds (204.1 to 449.1 kg)
- **Lifespan:** up to 20 years
- **Conservation Status:** Varies by species

HABITAT & DIET

Zebras prefer to eat grass, but they will also consume shrubs, twigs, and leaves. They inhabit a variety of habitats, including grasslands, woodlands, shrublands, and mountains.

FAMILY & SOCIAL LIFE

Zebras are prey for large predators such as lions and cheetahs, so they travel in herds for safety. Of the three zebra species, the Grevy's is the least social.

DID YOU KNOW?

Zebras' stripes were long thought to confuse predators, making it harder for them to target a single zebra. But the stripes' main function is to keep biting flies away, as these pests prefer to land on animals with solid hides.

Plains zebras

ALLEN'S SWAMP MONKEY

ALL ABOUT

Unlike most monkeys, Allen's swamp monkey is a strong swimmer. It spends most of its time in trees but will venture into the water to escape predators or search for food. This small but stout monkey has grayish-green fur that grows longer around its face and neck.

- **Height:** up to 18 inches (45.7 cm)
- **Weight:** 8 to 13 pounds (3.6 to 5.9 kg)
- **Lifespan:** up to 28 years
- **Conservation Status:** Least Concern

FUN FACT

These monkeys have webbed fingers and toes, which help them swim.

HABITAT & DIET

The Allen's swamp monkey lives in swamp forests. Fruit makes up most of its diet. It will also consume fish, insects, and other small prey.

AYE-AYE

ALL ABOUT

The aye-aye is a type of lemur, a family of primates found only on the island of Madagascar. It has dark gray-brown fur and a long, bushy tail. Its extra-long middle fingers are used to probe tree crevices for food.

- **Length:** 12 to 16 inches (30.5 to 40.6 cm)
- **Weight:** 5 to 6 pounds (2.3 to 2.7 kg)
- **Lifespan:** up to 20 years
- **Conservation Status:** Endangered

DID YOU KNOW?

The aye-aye uses percussive foraging to feed. It taps on trees and listens for activity inside. Once it hears movement, the aye-aye gnaws through or pulls off the bark to get its meal.

HABITAT & DIET

The aye-aye sleeps in nests made of leaves and twigs, emerging at night to find insect larvae, such as grubs. In addition to grubs, it eats nuts, fruit, seeds, and nectar.

FAMILY & SOCIAL LIFE

Aye-ayes are solitary, but they will sometimes share overlapping territory.

BARBARY MACAQUE

ALL ABOUT

The Barbary macaque has thick yellowish-brown to gray fur and pale underparts. The Barbary macaque's tail is small and mostly hidden by fur. As a result, the Barbary macaque is sometimes mistakenly called a Barbary "ape," as apes do not have tails.

- **Length:** 24 inches (61 cm)
- **Weight:** 24.3 to 35 pounds (11 to 15.9 kg)
- **Lifespan:** up to 20 years
- **Conservation Status:** Endangered

HABITAT & DIET

These monkeys live in forests, grasslands, scrublands, and cliffs. They eat fruit, plants, seeds, invertebrates, and lizards.

FUN FACT

The Barbary macaque is the only macaque species that lives outside of Asia.

FAMILY & SOCIAL LIFE

They live in large groups with multiple males, females, and offspring.

BONOBO

ALL ABOUT

Bonobos are great apes, along with gorillas, chimpanzees, and orangutans. They resemble chimpanzees but have slighter builds and darker faces. These intelligent primates live in complex communities. They have a peaceful nature.

- **Height:** 3.8 feet (1.2 m)
- **Weight:** 68 to 86 pounds (30.8 to 39 kg)
- **Lifespan:** up to 40 years
- **Conservation Status:** Endangered

HABITAT & DIET

Bonobos are only found in the rainforests of the Democratic Republic of the Congo. They are omnivores, eating fruit, leaves, honey, and insects.

FAMILY & SOCIAL LIFE

Bonobos live in large mixed-gender groups.

DID YOU KNOW?

The Bonobo Peace Forest is a network of forest preserves in the Congo that safeguards bonobos. Community members manage the forest, protecting the apes and other wildlife.

CHIMPANZEE

ALL ABOUT

Chimpanzees, also called chimps, are often mistaken for monkeys, but these tailless primates are great apes. The chimpanzee has dark skin covered with long black hair that grays with age. Its arms are longer than its legs. Females are slightly smaller than males. Chimps have opposable thumbs and big toes that allow them to grasp objects and use tools.

- **Height:** 3.5 to 5 feet (1.1 to 1.5 m)
- **Weight:** 70 to 120 pounds (31.8 to 54.4 kg)
- **Lifespan:** up to 40 years
- **Conservation Status:** Endangered

FUN FACT

Chimpanzees and humans share more than 98 percent of their DNA.

HABITAT & DIET

Chimpanzees primarily live in forests and grasslands. They are omnivores, with fruit, leaves, and nuts making up the bulk of their diet. Insects and other animal prey provide additional sources of food. Chimps spend their days searching for food. At night, they build individual nests high in the forest canopy.

FAMILY & SOCIAL LIFE

Chimpanzees live in large troops of up to 100 individuals led by a dominant male. Smaller subgroups periodically leave and rejoin the larger troop. This type of social structure is called fission-fusion. Chimpanzees are highly territorial, and interactions between troops are usually aggressive.

DID YOU KNOW?

The chimpanzee was the first non-human species observed to make and use tools.

Red colobus monkey

COLOBUS MONKEY

ALL ABOUT

Colobus monkeys are divided into three groups based on their color: black-and-white, red, and olive. Colobus monkeys have multi-chambered stomachs to break down leaves.

- **Height:** 16 to 28 inches (40.6 to 71.1 cm)
- **Weight:** 4.5 to 30 pounds (2 to 13.6 kg)
- **Lifespan:** up to 20 years
- **Conservation Status:** Varies by species

HABITAT & DIET

Colobus monkeys must eat a lot of leaves to get enough calories. They mostly feed high in the forest canopy.

FAMILY & SOCIAL LIFE

Colobus monkeys live in groups of up to 15 monkeys led by a dominant male.

Black-and-white colobus monkey

DE BRAZZA'S MONKEY

ALL ABOUT

The De Brazza's monkey has a white beard and a crescent-shaped crown of orange fur on its head. It has a speckled grayish coat with black arms and legs. These monkeys spend more time on the ground than in trees.

- **Length:** 19 to 24 inches (48.3 to 61 cm)
- **Weight:** 15 to 18 pounds (6.8 to 8.2 kg)
- **Lifespan:** up to 22 years
- **Conservation Status:** Least Concern

FUN FACT

These monkeys have pouches in their cheeks, which they use to store food.

HABITAT & DIET

De Brazza's monkeys inhabit swamp forests and bamboo forests. Fruit, seeds, and leaves make up the bulk of their diet.

FAMILY & SOCIAL LIFE

Groups often consist of a pair and their offspring. Some males lead larger groups.

GALAGO

ALL ABOUT

There are at least 20 different species of galagos. These small, nocturnal primates are also known as bush babies. The "bush baby" nickname comes from the vocalization made by some species, which sounds like a crying infant. Galagos have big eyes and bushy tails. Their ears have ridges and can bend to pinpoint sound.

- **Length:** 2.9 to 15.8 inches (7.4 to 40.1 cm)
- **Weight:** 1.2 ounces to 4 pounds (34 g to 1.8 kg)
- **Lifespan:** 3 to 4 years
- **Conservation Status:** Varies by species

HABITAT & DIET

Galagos sleep in natural tree hollows or construct nests in tree forks. They eat whatever is readily available, including insects, leaves, fruit, and sap.

FAMILY & SOCIAL LIFE

They live in pairs or small family groups.

FUN FACT

Galagos use urine to mark themselves and their territory.

GELADA MONKEY

ALL ABOUT

Gelada monkeys have long, thick coats that insulate them from the cold temperatures of the mountains. Males are much larger than females.

- **Height:** 20 to 29 inches (50.8 to 73.7 cm)
- **Weight:** 41.9 to 46 pounds (19 to 20.9 kg)
- **Lifespan:** up to 20 years
- **Conservation Status:** Least Concern

HABITAT & DIET

These monkeys are only found in the highlands of Ethiopia. They sleep on cliff ledges. Grass makes up 90 percent of their diet.

FAMILY & SOCIAL LIFE

Gelada monkeys live in small family groups but will band together in herds of 100 or more. They spend a few hours each morning grooming one another. This ritual strengthens social bonds.

DID YOU KNOW?

Like most African monkeys, geladas have thick pads of tissue on their bottoms to help them spend long hours sitting on hard ground.

Western lowland gorilla

GORILLA

ALL ABOUT

Gorillas are the strongest and largest of the great apes. Male gorillas beat their chest to communicate their size and strength. Although able to stand and walk bipedally for short periods, gorillas normally walk on all fours. They curl their fingers under and put pressure on their knuckles. This form of locomotion is called knuckle walking.

There are two gorilla species, Eastern and Western, which are each broken into two subspecies. The Grauer's gorilla is the largest, and the Western lowland is the smallest. There are fewer than 300 Cross River gorillas believed to remain on Earth. The fourth subspecies is the mountain gorilla.

- **Height:** 4.5 to 6 feet (1.4 to 1.8 m)
- **Weight:** 160 to 550 pounds (72.6 to 249.5 kg)
- **Lifespan:** 35 to 40 years
- **Conservation Status:** Critically Endangered

HABITAT & DIET

Gorillas are classified as omnivores, but they mostly eat plant matter. Their diet depends on their habitat. Western lowland gorillas eat fruit when it is available, whereas mountain gorillas eat a higher percentage of leaves.

FAMILY & SOCIAL LIFE

A gorilla troop consists of multiple males, females, and young. It is led by a dominant male called a silverback.

FUN FACT

Biologists studying gorillas can tell them apart by their nose prints. No two are alike.

Mountain gorillas

HAMADRYAS BABOON

ALL ABOUT

Baboons are large, terrestrial monkeys. The Hamadryas baboon has a thick, silver-gray coat, a bare pink face and backside, and a short tail. Males have a heavy mane. Powerful jaws and large canine teeth give baboons a fierce appearance.

- **Height:** 1.5 to 3.1 feet (0.5 to 0.9 m)
- **Weight:** 22 to 48 pounds (10 to 21.8 kg)
- **Lifespan:** up to 20 years
- **Conservation Status:** Least Concern

HABITAT & DIET

Baboons prefer open savannas, hillsides, and rocky areas. As omnivores, they eat a wide range of vegetation and animal prey.

FAMILY & SOCIAL LIFE

These baboons live in complex societies in which huge troops are made of smaller subgroups. A strict hierarchy is followed, with males dominating females.

FUN FACT

Hamadryas baboons were kept as pets by ancient Egyptians, who sometimes mummified their remains.

INDRI

ALL ABOUT

The indri is the largest lemur species. It is black with white patches and a short, stumpy tail. Its coloring varies depending on its region. Southern populations have more white fur, whereas those that live in the north are nearly all black. Indris are known for their loud, rhythmic calls.

- **Length:** 2.1 to 2.4 feet (0.6 to 0.7 m)
- **Weight:** 13 to 21 pounds (5.9 to 9.5 kg)
- **Lifespan:** 15 to 18 years
- **Conservation Status:** Critically Endangered

HABITAT & DIET

Like all lemurs, the indri is only found on the island of Madagascar. It inhabits tropical forests and dines mostly on leaves and flowers.

FAMILY & SOCIAL LIFE

Indris live in pairs with their offspring. Females are dominant over males.

FUN FACT

The indri is known in Madagascar as *babakoto*, meaning "old man."

MANDRILL

ALL ABOUT

The mandrill is one of the largest and most colorful monkey species. Males have bright red-and-blue faces and similarly colored rumps.

- **Height:** 1.5 to 3 feet (0.5 to 0.9 m)
- **Weight:** 28.7 to 77.2 pounds (13 to 35 kg)
- **Lifespan:** up to 20 years
- **Conservation Status:** Vulnerable

HABITAT & DIET

Mandrills inhabit rainforests, spending their days on the ground and sleeping in trees at night. They are omnivores, primarily eating fruit and seeds. They also consume leaves, bark, eggs, fungi, and small animal prey.

DID YOU KNOW?

The mandrill exhibits sexual dimorphism, which means males and females of the same species appear extremely different. Female mandrills are about one-third the size of males, and their faces are much paler.

FAMILY & SOCIAL LIFE

Mandrills live in troops of a few dozen to more than 200 members. They are led by a dominant male.

MOUSE LEMUR

ALL ABOUT

Mouse lemurs are small members of the lemur family and are the smallest primates on Earth. They have short limbs and long tails. Large eyes help these nocturnal animals see at night.

- **Length:** 2.25 to 4.75 inches (5.7 to 12.1 cm)
- **Weight:** 1 to 4 ounces (28.3 to 113.4 g)
- **Lifespan:** 10 to 12 years
- **Conservation Status:** Vulnerable

HABITAT & DIET

Mouse lemurs live in forest habitats. During the day, they sleep in tree cavities or nests. At night, they forage for insects, fruit, flowers, and nectar.

FAMILY & SOCIAL LIFE

Mouse lemurs are solitary during their active nighttime hours. They come together to sleep in groups during the day. Females are dominant over males.

FUN FACT

The smallest lemur, Madame Berthe's mouse lemur weighs less than a golf ball.

FUN FACT

This monkey likely inspired Dr. Seuss's character, the Lorax.

PATAS MONKEY

ALL ABOUT

Able to reach speeds of up to 34 miles per hour (54.7 kmh), the patas monkey is the world's fastest primate. It has reddish-brown fur with white extremities, belly, and facial hair.

- **Height:** 23.5 to 35 inches (59.7 to 88.9 cm)
- **Weight:** 9 to 29 pounds (4.1 to 13.2 kg)
- **Lifespan:** 15 to 20 years
- **Conservation Status:** Near Threatened

HABITAT & DIET

These monkeys inhabit woodlands and savannas. They spend their days on the ground but sleep in trees to avoid predators. They eat gum from acacia trees, as well as leaves, insects, fruit, and seeds.

FAMILY & SOCIAL LIFE

A patas monkey troop usually consists of one male and multiple females and offspring. The male will protect the troop and chase other males away.

POTTO

ALL ABOUT

Pottos are members of the primate family, more closely related to lemurs than monkeys. They are nocturnal and arboreal. Slow moving, they can remain still for hours to avoid attracting attention. Pottos have spiny neck vertebrae that form a kind of protective shield.

DID YOU KNOW?

A potto mother will leave her infant in a tree overnight while she forages. This practice is known as infant parking.

- **Length:** 12 to 16 inches (30.5 to 40.6 cm)
- **Weight:** 1.8 to 3.3 pounds (0.8 to 1.5 kg)
- **Lifespan:** up to 26 years (under human care)
- **Conservation Status:** Near Threatened

HABITAT & DIET

Pottos inhabit rainforests and savannas. They stay high in the canopy, rarely descending from the trees. Fruit and insects are this primate's preferred foods.

FAMILY & SOCIAL LIFE

Other than females with their young, pottos lead largely solitary lives.

RING-TAILED LEMUR

ALL ABOUT

The ring-tail lemur is easily recognized by its striped tail, which is longer than its body. It is arboreal but spends a great deal of time on the ground. It holds its tail in the air while traveling. Troop members stay together by following the leader's tail. Lemurs have a special row of teeth on their bottom jaw called a tooth comb, which they use to groom their fur. Ring-tailed lemurs have scent glands on their wrists and chests.

- **Length:** 15 to 18 inches (38.1 to 45.7 cm)
- **Weight:** 5 to 8 pounds (2.3 to 3.6 kg)
- **Lifespan:** 16 to 18 years
- **Conservation Status:** Endangered

HABITAT & DIET

Ring-tail lemurs live in scrublands and forests of Madagascar. They prefer fruit but also eat leaves, flowers, seeds, insects, and sap.

FAMILY & SOCIAL LIFE

Ring-tailed lemurs live in large troops in which all females are dominant. Females remain in the troop they were born into. Males leave and join other troops.

DID YOU KNOW?

When competing for females, male ring-tailed lemurs engage in stink fights. They rub secretions from their scent glands onto their tails. Then they flick their tails at each other.

FUN FACT

Lemurs keep forests healthy by eating fruit and dispersing seeds in their poop.

SIFAKA

ALL ABOUT

The sifaka is a type of lemur that maintains a vertical posture as it leaps between trees. On the ground, sifakas don't walk but bounce on two legs. They use their tail and arms for balance. Sifakas are mostly white with brown patches on their chests, arms, and sides.

- **Height:** 16 to 20 inches (40.6 to 50.8 cm)
- **Weight:** 8 to 9 pounds (3.6 to 4.1 kg)
- **Lifespan:** up to 30 years
- **Conservation Status:** Critically Endangered

HABITAT & DIET

Sifakas inhabit forests and scrublands in Madagascar. They predominantly eat leaves, fruit, flowers, and bark.

FAMILY & SOCIAL LIFE

A sifaka group consists of 2 to 10 individuals. As with most other types of lemurs, females are dominant.

VERVET MONKEY

ALL ABOUT

Vervet monkeys are widespread in East Africa. This medium-sized monkey has a whitish-gray coat and a long tail. Its black face is surrounded by white fur. Males are larger than females.

- **Length:** 1.3 to 2 feet (0.4 to 0.6 m)
- **Weight:** 8 to 18 pounds (3.6 to 8.2 kg)
- **Lifespan:** 12 to 15 years
- **Conservation Status:** Least Concern

FUN FACT

These monkeys make different alarm calls to communicate different types of danger.

HABITAT & DIET

These adaptable monkeys are found in a wide range of habitats, often near rivers or lakes. They are omnivores, with leaves, flowers, and fruit dominating their diet.

FAMILY & SOCIAL LIFE

Vervet monkeys live in large mixed-gender groups. All the females in a troop help care for infants.

AFRICAN SAVANNA HARE

ALL ABOUT

The African savanna hare is grayish brown with white underparts. This coloring provides excellent camouflage in dry landscapes. The hare's long ears can move independently to detect predators. Powerful hind legs help it leap great distances.

- **Length:** 16 to 23 inches (40.6 to 58.4 cm)
- **Weight:** 3 to 7 pounds (1.4 to 3.2 kg)
- **Lifespan:** up to 5 years
- **Conservation Status:** Least Concern

FUN FACT

The African savanna hare runs in a zigzag pattern when frightened.

HABITAT & DIET

This hare inhabits grasslands, savannas, and scrublands. Active at night, it spends the day resting under bushes or in depressions in the ground. It eats leaves, roots, berries, and bark.

FAMILY & SOCIAL LIFE

This species is mainly solitary, though it will sometimes forage in small groups.

CAPE PORCUPINE

ALL ABOUT

The Cape porcupine is a large rodent. Its quills are made of keratin. Contrary to myth, a porcupine cannot shoot its quills. If threatened, it will turn and back into an opponent to deliver a sharp jab.

- **Length:** 25 to 32 inches (63.5 to 81.3 cm)
- **Weight:** 40 to 60 pounds (18.1 to 27.2 kg)
- **Lifespan:** 12 to 15 years
- **Conservation Status:** Least Concern

HABITAT & DIET

Cape porcupines occupy a wide range of habitats and will eat whatever vegetation is available. They shelter in caves, rock crevices, or burrows.

DID YOU KNOW?

The Cape porcupine is an ecosystem engineer, which is a species that significantly modifies its environment. Its extensive digging alters soil and plant composition. Its habit of gnawing rings around trees can turn woodlands into savannas.

FAMILY & SOCIAL LIFE

Cape porcupines live singly or in pairs with their offspring.

GUNDI

ALL ABOUT

Gundis look somewhat like guinea pigs, but they are not closely related. The gundi has big eyes, sharp claws, and gray or brown fur. When temperatures rise, these desert dwellers will flatten their bodies against cool surfaces. Their sharp whistles warn of predators.

- **Length:** 6.3 to 9.4 inches (16 to 23.9 cm)
- **Weight:** 6 to 7 ounces (170.1 to 198.4 g)
- **Lifespan:** 3 to 4 years
- **Conservation Status:** Least Concern

DID YOU KNOW?

A conservation status of "least concern" does not mean scientists are not concerned. This status means these species have a lower risk of extinction, though some may be declining.

HABITAT & DIET

Gundis are found only in rocky deserts. They shelter in rocks and caves. They eat seeds, leaves, flowers, and other vegetation.

FAMILY & SOCIAL LIFE

Gundis live in colonies that can be large or small, depending on their location and food availability.

JERBOA

ALL ABOUT

The jerboa looks like a long-legged mouse but hops like a kangaroo. This desert rodent can leap up to 10 feet (3 m), propelled by its long, springy hind legs. There are several species of jerboa in Africa. The long-eared jerboa's ears can be half the length of its body.

- **Length:** 1.7 to 7.1 inches (4.3 to 18 cm)
- **Weight:** 0.1 to 12 ounces (2.8 to 340.2 g)
- **Lifespan:** up to 6 years
- **Conservation Status:** Varies by species

HABITAT & DIET

Jerboas rest in burrows during the day and emerge at night to dine on seeds, insects, and plants.

FAMILY & SOCIAL LIFE

Jerboas are mostly solitary.

FUN FACT

Jerboas rapidly change their manner and direction of movement to confuse predators.

NAKED MOLE-RAT

ALL ABOUT

Naked mole-rats are more closely related to guinea pigs than they are to moles or rats. These rodents have powerful jaws and long, sharp teeth. Fine hairs on their body help them sense their environment, much like whiskers do. They have tiny eyes but are practically blind.

The naked mole-rat's average body temperature changes with its environment. So, despite being a mammal, it is essentially cold-blooded, like a reptile. Since they cannot produce their own body heat, naked mole-rats often huddle in a pile for warmth.

- **Length:** 3 to 4 inches (7.6 to 10.2 cm)
- **Weight:** 1 to 2.5 ounces (28.3 to 70.9 g)
- **Lifespan:** up to 30 years
- **Conservation Status:** Least Concern

FUN FACT

The naked mole-rat lives longer than any other rodent.

HABITAT & DIET

These animals live in complex underground burrows in grassland habitats. They eat the underground parts of plants.

FAMILY & SOCIAL LIFE

Like ants or bees, naked mole-rats live in large colonies centered around a single dominant female. Most other group members are workers whose jobs shift as they grow. The queen can have 50 or more babies in a year.

DID YOU KNOW?

Naked mole-rats rarely get diseases such as cancer or diabetes. Scientists are studying these animals to gain information that could be used to prevent these diseases in humans.

POUCHED RAT

ALL ABOUT

Pouched rats have large pouches in their cheeks that they stuff with food. The biggest pouched rats are about the size of a small cat. These rodents have poor eyesight but an excellent sense of smell.

- **Length:** up to 16 inches (40.6 cm)
- **Weight:** up to 6.6 pounds (3 kg)
- **Lifespan:** 7 to 9 years
- **Conservation Status:** Least Concern

FUN FACT

Giant pouched rats have been trained to detect landmines, saving many lives.

HABITAT & DIET

Pouched rats are omnivores. Their preferred foods include fruit, insects, and nuts. They dig burrows in moist soil or nest in hollow trees. They inhabit forests, woodlands, and agricultural fields.

FAMILY & SOCIAL LIFE

Pouched rats tend to be solitary, but they sometimes live in groups.

SPRINGHARE

ALL ABOUT

The springhare is not a hare but a large rodent. It moves bipedally, jumping on its long, hind legs while holding its short forelegs close to its body. Its body color ranges from yellow brown to reddish.

- **Length:** 13 to 18 inches (33 to 45.7 cm)
- **Weight:** 6.5 to 9 pounds (2.9 to 4.1 kg)
- **Lifespan:** up to 10 years
- **Conservation Status:** Least Concern

FUN FACT

Springhares are biofluorescent, a rare trait among mammals. They glow under ultraviolet light.

HABITAT & DIET

Springhares live in savannas and semi-deserts. They spend their days in underground burrows, coming out at night to graze on grass and roots.

FAMILY & SOCIAL LIFE

They live in small family groups. Multiple families may live in adjoining burrows.

ADDITIONAL MAMMALS

AARDVARK

ALL ABOUT

The aardvark has a pig-like snout, donkey-like ears, bear-like claws, and an anteater-like tongue for slurping up insects. It is not closely related to any of these species, but is the only member of its own order of mammals.

- **Length:** 3 to 5 feet (0.9 to 1.5 m)
- **Weight:** 88 to 181 pounds (39.9 to 82.1 kg)
- **Lifespan:** up to 18 years
- **Conservation Status:** Least Concern

DID YOU KNOW?

Aardvarks create new burrows frequently. Abandoned burrows serve as homes for other animals. This large impact on the environment makes aardvarks a keystone species.

HABITAT & DIET

Aardvarks inhabit savannas, grasslands, and woodlands. They live in extensive burrows, which they excavate themselves. Nocturnal, they sleep by day and hunt for ants, termites, and larvae at night.

AFRICAN CIVET

ALL ABOUT

The African civet is the largest civet species, a type of feliform or cat-like carnivore. Its long body is covered with spots and stripes. It has black bands around its eyes and a short black mane that runs along its spine. This mane can stand up when the civet is agitated, helping it to appear larger.

- **Length:** 16 to 34 inches (40.6 to 86.4 cm)
- **Weight:** 15 to 44 pounds (6.8 to 20 kg)
- **Lifespan:** 15 to 20 years
- **Conservation Status:** Least Concern

HABITAT & DIET

The African civet occupies savannas and forests. Its diet is broad and undiscriminating. It will even eat rotting carcasses and toxic species avoided by other animals.

FAMILY & SOCIAL LIFE

Civets are mostly solitary.

FUN FACT

Civets produce a strong-smelling musk, which they use to mark their territory.

FOSSA

ALL ABOUT

The fossa is a muscular feliform with a dark brown coat. Retractable claws and flexible ankle joints help it move swiftly through trees in pursuit of arboreal prey. A long tail helps with balance.

- **Length:** 27 to 31 inches (68.6 to 78.7 cm)
- **Weight:** 12 to 19 pounds (5.4 to 8.6 kg)
- **Lifespan:** up to 15 years
- **Conservation Status:** Vulnerable

HABITAT & DIET

The fossa only lives on Madagascar, where it is the island's largest predator. Its prey includes lemurs, pigs, and rodents.

FUN FACT

Fossas are cathemeral, meaning they can be active at any time of the day or night.

FAMILY & SOCIAL LIFE

Fossas are solitary animals.

FUN FACT

When threatened, genets produce warning sounds, such as a growl, hiss, or click.

GENET

ALL ABOUT

A genet is a feliform with a long body, short legs, and a long, bushy tail. Its coat is grayish with dark spots and stripes. It can squeeze its flexible body through small openings, an advantage when hunting.

- **Length:** 16 to 24 inches (40.6 to 61 cm)
- **Weight:** 2 to 7 pounds (0.9 to 3.2 kg)
- **Lifespan:** 8 to 10 years
- **Conservation Status:** Varies by species

HABITAT & DIET

Genets are able to adapt to a variety of habitats, including deserts, forests, grasslands, and mountainous regions. They eat small mammals, birds, reptiles, and insects.

FAMILY & SOCIAL LIFE

Genets are solitary except when mating or raising young.

HAMMER-HEADED BAT

ALL ABOUT

The hammer-headed bat can have a wingspan of up to 3 feet (0.9 m). Males have a large snout that amplifies its mating call. Females are much smaller, with compact faces.

- **Length:** 8 to 11 inches (20.3 to 27.9 cm)
- **Weight:** 8 to 16 ounces (226.8 to 453.6 g)
- **Lifespan:** up to 30 years
- **Conservation Status:** Least Concern

HABITAT & DIET

A type of fruit bat, the hammer-headed bat eats figs, mangos, guavas, and other fruit. It roosts high in the canopy of tropical forests, especially near rivers and swamps.

FAMILY & SOCIAL LIFE

When competing for females, males hang from branches and honk noisily. Females pick their preferred partner based on his calls.

FUN FACT

Fruit bats, also known as megabats, are larger than insect-eating bats.

HONEY BADGER

ALL ABOUT

The honey badger is a small member of the weasel family. It is known for its aggressive attitude. It will even stand up to lions and leopards.

- **Length:** 29 to 38 inches (73.7 to 96.5 cm)
- **Weight:** 13.6 to 30 pounds (6.2 to 13.6 kg)
- **Lifespan:** up to 24 years
- **Conservation Status:** Least Concern

HABITAT & DIET

True to its name, the honey badger is fond of honey, especially the bee larvae contained inside. It also eats fruit and animal prey, including snakes and scorpions. Honey badgers sleep in burrows that they usually steal from another animal rather than dig themselves.

FAMILY & SOCIAL LIFE

These animals are solitary. A cub stays with its mother for about a year.

FUN FACT

Thick, loose skin protects the honey badger against snake bites and insect stings.

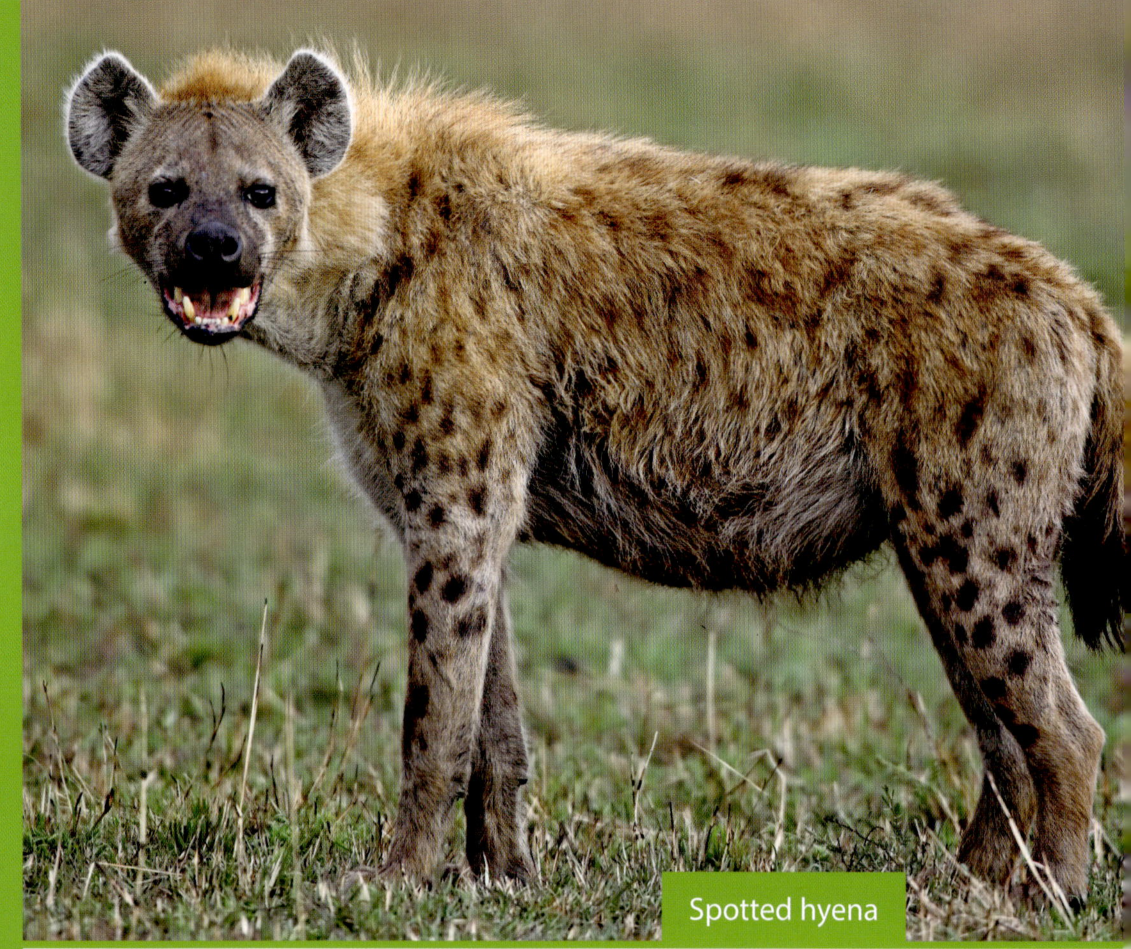

Spotted hyena

HYENA

ALL ABOUT

The hyena family has four members: the spotted hyena, the brown hyena, the striped hyena, and the aardwolf. These powerful carnivores look like dogs but are more closely related to cats. Their colors and markings vary by species. Their ears are short and rounded. Their jaws and teeth are strong enough to crush bone. Hyenas are often thought of as scavengers, but they are also efficient hunters.

FUN FACT

Hyenas hide their leftovers. They often stash food underwater to hide the scent.

- **Length:** 3 to 5.5 feet (0.9 to 1.7 m)
- **Weight:** 49 to 190 pounds (22.2 to 86.1 kg)
- **Lifespan:** up to 25 years
- **Conservation Status:** Varies by species

HABITAT & DIET

Hyenas live in savannas, scrublands, and semi-deserts. They sleep in dens, often enlarging burrows made by warthogs or other animals. Aardwolves mainly eat termites. The other hyena species are not picky eaters, consuming a wide variety of prey.

FAMILY & SOCIAL LIFE

The striped hyena and aardwolf are mostly solitary. Brown and spotted hyenas live in large clans in which females outrank males.

Brown hyena

DID YOU KNOW?

Hyenas are associated with laughter, but only spotted hyenas make vocalizations that sound like human giggles. In these hyenas, "laughing" is usually a sign of fear or frustration.

MEERKAT

ALL ABOUT

Meerkats are small burrowing mammals with light brown fur and a pointed snout. They are known for their upright posture while scanning the skies for danger. Typically, one meerkat will be on guard duty while the rest of the group searches for food. Dark circles around the meerkat's eyes cut down glare from the sun.

- **Height:** 10 to 14 inches (25.4 to 35.6 cm)
- **Weight:** 1.4 to 2.1 pounds (0.6 to 1 kg)
- **Lifespan:** up to 15 years
- **Conservation Status:** Least Concern

HABITAT & DIET

Meerkats are found in deserts and grasslands. They create complex burrows with multiple entrances and exits. A group may have multiple burrows spread out over a large territory. The bulk of their diet is insects, but these omnivores will also eat fruit, eggs, rodents, birds, and reptiles.

FUN FACT

Meerkats have a natural immunity to scorpion venom.

FAMILY & SOCIAL LIFE

Meerkats live in large groups led by a dominant female. Other members take turns babysitting pups, finding food, and looking out for danger. They sleep huddled together for warmth.

MONGOOSE

ALL ABOUT

There are more than 30 mongoose species. They have long, slender bodies with shaggy hair and bushy tails. Some have stripes or bands. They are active during the day.

- **Length:** 7 to 28 inches (17.8 to 71.1 cm)
- **Weight:** 7 ounces to 9.2 pounds (0.2 to 4.2 kg)
- **Lifespan:** up to 14 years
- **Conservation Status:** Varies by species

HABITAT & DIET

Mongooses are found across most of Africa, occupying a wide range of habitats. They make their homes in burrows, tunnels, or rock crevices. They hunt small animals such as birds, rodents, amphibians, and insects. Some species also eat fruit and seeds.

FUN FACT

The mongoose is one of few animals that will challenge a king cobra and win.

FAMILY & SOCIAL LIFE

Mongoose social systems vary by species. The banded mongoose lives in groups of 15 to 20.

PANGOLIN

ALL ABOUT

Pangolins are the only mammals covered in scales, which are made of keratin. When it senses danger, a pangolin curls into a ball. Its sharp, overlapping scales form a protective shield. Four pangolin species live in Africa.

- **Length:** 12 to 71 inches (30.5 to 180.3 cm)
- **Weight:** 2.2 to 70 pounds (1 to 31.8 kg)
- **Lifespan:** up to 20 years
- **Conservation Status:** Varies by species

HABITAT & DIET

Pangolins live in trees or underground burrows, depending on the species. They inhabit forests, savannas, and grasslands. They use their long tongue to eat ants and termites. Strong claws help them break open termite mounds.

FAMILY & SOCIAL LIFE

Pangolins are solitary and nocturnal.

DID YOU KNOW?

Millions of pangolins have been killed due to the false belief that their scales have medicinal or magical properties.

STRIPED POLECAT

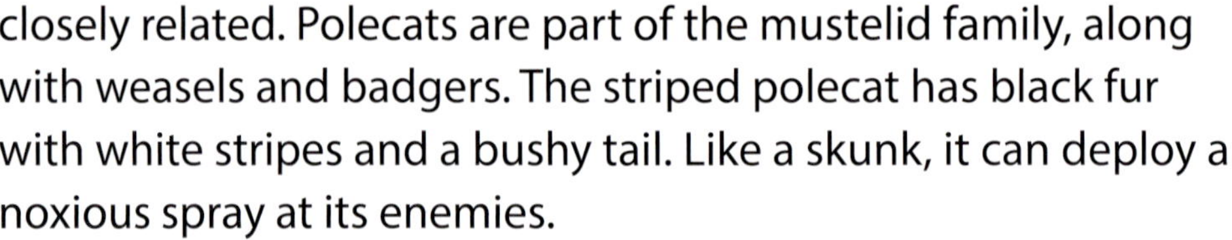

ALL ABOUT

The striped polecat looks like a skunk, but the two are not closely related. Polecats are part of the mustelid family, along with weasels and badgers. The striped polecat has black fur with white stripes and a bushy tail. Like a skunk, it can deploy a noxious spray at its enemies.

- **Length:** 11 to 11.8 inches (27.9 to 30 cm)
- **Weight:** 2.2 to 3 pounds (1 to 1.4 kg)
- **Lifespan:** about 6 years
- **Conservation Status:** Least Concern

HABITAT & DIET

The striped polecat lives in deserts, forests, and grasslands. Its prey includes small reptiles, rodents, frogs, and birds.

FUN FACT

The striped polecat's nickname, zorilla, means "little fox."

FAMILY & SOCIAL LIFE

Striped polecats are solitary and territorial. They use scent to mark their territory and warn others to stay away.

TENREC

ALL ABOUT

About 30 species of tenrecs exist. Some resemble hedgehogs. Others look like mice or shrews. These small nocturnal mammals are native to Madagascar. Many tenrecs hibernate or enter a period of dormancy for several months at a time when food resources are limited.

- **Length:** 1.8 to 15.3 inches (4.6 to 38.9 cm)
- **Weight:** 0.1 ounces to 2.2 pounds (2.8 g to 1 kg)
- **Lifespan:** up to 10 years
- **Conservation Status:** Least Concern

HABITAT & DIET

Tenrecs mostly eat invertebrates. Some tenrecs also eat fruit, eggs, and small vertebrates. Tenrecs live in a variety of habitats. Some live in trees, and others create underground burrows. The web-footed tenrec is semiaquatic.

FAMILY & SOCIAL LIFE

Most tenrecs are solitary, but the streaked tenrec lives in groups of up to 20.

FUN FACT

Streaked tenrecs rub their spines together to produce sound, a form of communication called stridulation.

Atlantic humpback dolphin

ATLANTIC HUMPBACK DOLPHIN

- **About:** These dolphins prefer to stay close to shore.
- **Habitat:** tropical coastal waters
- **Conservation Status:** Critically Endangered

Desert hedgehog

DESERT HEDGEHOG

- **About:** This hedgehog can survive extreme heat and long periods of drought.
- **Habitat:** deserts
- **Conservation Status:** Least Concern

DIK-DIK

- **About:** This tiny antelope is just over 1 foot (0.3 m) tall.
- **Habitat:** shrublands, savannas
- **Conservation Status:** Least Concern

Dik-dik

SABLE ANTELOPE

- **About:** The sable antelope's huge horns curve backward.
- **Habitat:** savannas, woodlands
- **Conservation Status:** Least Concern

SITATUNGA

- **About:** This swamp-dwelling antelope is an excellent swimmer.
- **Habitat:** swamps, marshes
- **Conservation Status:** Least Concern

STRIPED GRASS MOUSE

- **About:** Stripes help this mouse camouflage in grass.
- **Habitat:** grasslands, woodlands, forests
- **Conservation Status:** Least Concern

Sable antelope

Sitatunga

Striped grass mouse

REPTILES

Reptiles vary greatly in terms of size and behavior. Most have thick outer skin with scales. Some also have crests, shells, or other protective structures. Different species have different modes of locomotion depending on their habitat and diet. They may climb, crawl, slither, swim, leap, run, or glide. They tend to move slowly in cold weather and more quickly when temperatures are warm.

Africa is home to giant reptiles such as the Nile crocodile and the Aldabra tortoise. It is also home to the smallest reptiles on Earth: the dime-sized chameleons in the *Brookesia* genus. Reptiles prefer to live in warm temperatures. Thus, reptile biodiversity is high across equatorial Africa. Fewer species are found at high elevations.

Giant ground geckos live in southern Africa.

African spurred tortoises live in the Sahara Desert.

WHAT IS A REPTILE?

- Reptiles are vertebrates. This means they have a backbone.
- They are cold-blooded. They don't produce their own body heat.
- Most lay eggs. A few give birth to live young.
- They have scales rather than hair or feathers.

CROCODILES

ALL ABOUT

Crocodiles are found in tropical waters around the world. These semiaquatic predators have thick skin, powerful tails, and long, pointed snouts.

Five species are found in Africa. At about 5 feet (1.5 m) long, the dwarf crocodile is the world's smallest crocodile. The Nile crocodile is the second largest, ranking just behind Australia's saltwater croc. The West African crocodile, West African slender-snouted crocodile, and Central African slender-snouted crocodile fall in between in size. The two slender-snouted crocodiles are critically endangered.

- **Length:** 5 to 20 feet (1.5 to 6.1 m)
- **Weight:** 39 to 1,500 pounds (17.7 to 680.4 kg)
- **Lifespan:** up to 45 years
- **Conservation Status:** Varies by species

FUN FACT

When they are ready to hatch, crocodile babies chirp to get their mother's attention.

Nile crocodile

African dwarf crocodile

HABITAT & DIET

Africa's crocodiles live in freshwater swamps, marshes, rivers, and lakes. They mostly eat fish but will attack nearly any animal that comes close, including buffalo and wildebeest.

DID YOU KNOW?

The Nile crocodile lets birds pick leftover food from its mouth. The birds keep the crocodile's teeth clean, and in exchange, the crocodile doesn't eat them.

FAMILY & SOCIAL LIFE

Unlike most reptiles, crocodiles care for their young. A Nile crocodile mother guards her nest, helps her babies hatch, and looks after them for the first few months. Crocodiles are somewhat solitary but will gather in groups to bask in the sun. Males will fight for the best territory.

AGAMA LIZARD

DID YOU KNOW?

Agamas can drop or amputate their own tails to escape predators. The tail regrows, but slowly, and often not completely.

ALL ABOUT

Male agama lizards turn bright colors to attract females. Outside of the mating season, a male's colors are more subdued. Females are always a drab brown or gray.

- **Length:** 5 to 18 inches (12.7 to 45.7 cm)
- **Weight:** up to 2 pounds (0.9 kg)
- **Lifespan:** up to 12 years
- **Conservation Status:** Varies by species

HABITAT & DIET

These lizards prefer rocky deserts. Most species are ground dwelling, but some are arboreal. They primarily eat insects.

FAMILY & SOCIAL LIFE

Agamas tend to live in social groups. The most colorful male is usually dominant. These lizards spend a lot of time basking in the sun, with the dominant male getting the highest rock.

ARMADILLO LIZARD

ALL ABOUT

To escape a predator, the slow-moving armadillo lizard bites its own tail. In this position, its soft stomach is protected. It can remain curled up for an hour or more, which is long enough for a hungry bird to give up and search for another meal.

- **Length:** 6 to 8 inches (15.2 to 20.3 cm)
- **Weight:** 2.5 to 3.5 ounces (70.9 to 99.2 g)
- **Lifespan:** up to 25 years
- **Conservation Status:** Near Threatened

FUN FACT

This lizard was named after the armadillo, which curls into a ball for protection.

HABITAT & DIET

These lizards live in deserts and scrublands. They hide in rock crevices and are often found near termite mounds. They mostly eat termites and other insects.

FAMILY & SOCIAL LIFE

Armadillo lizards are often found in groups of a dozen or more.

FAT-TAILED GECKO

ALL ABOUT

This gecko has a tan-and-brown body. It stores fat in its tail.

- **Length:** 6 to 10 inches (15.2 to 25.4 cm)
- **Weight:** 1.5 to 2.5 ounces (42.5 to 70.9 g)
- **Lifespan:** 15 to 20 years (under human care)
- **Conservation Status:** Least Concern

HABITAT & DIET

This species lives in woodlands, savannas, and rocky slopes. It hunts for insects at night.

JACKSON'S CHAMELEON

ALL ABOUT

This chameleon has three bony horns jutting out from its head. Males use them to compete with other males.

- **Length:** 7 to 10 inches (17.8 to 25.4 cm)
- **Weight:** 3.2 to 5.3 ounces (90.7 to 150.3 g)
- **Lifespan:** 2 to 3 years
- **Conservation Status:** Least Concern

HABITAT & DIET

They live in mountains and forests of eastern Africa and eat insects.

FAMILY & SOCIAL LIFE

A female may give birth to up to 50 live babies at a time.

LEAF-TAILED GECKO

ALL ABOUT

The leaf-tailed gecko's body and tail are shaped like leaves. It can change its skin color to match branches and bark. It has sticky toes and a broad, flat tail. This gecko can snap off its tail to distract predators. A new tail regrows.

- **Length:** 4 to 12 inches (10.2 to 30.5 cm)
- **Weight:** up to 1 ounce (28.3 g)
- **Lifespan:** up to 10 years
- **Conservation Status:** Least Concern

HABITAT & DIET

Leaf-tailed geckos live in dense tropical forests. They are only found on Madagascar and nearby islands. They eat a variety of invertebrates, including spiders, insects, and worms.

FAMILY & SOCIAL LIFE

Females lay up to three clutches of eggs per year. Each clutch has two to three eggs. When feeling threatened, the leaf-tailed gecko will open and display its bright red mouth and then emit a loud scream.

NILE MONITOR LIZARD

ALL ABOUT

The Nile monitor lizard is Africa's longest lizard, growing up to 8 feet (2.4 m) long. It has a muscular body and sharp claws. Usually found near water, it is an excellent climber and a strong swimmer.

- **Length:** 4 to 8 feet (1.2 to 2.4 m)
- **Weight:** 13 to 40 pounds (5.9 to 18.1 kg)
- **Lifespan:** 10 to 20 years
- **Conservation Status:** Least Concern

HABITAT & DIET

These lizards live in a variety of habitats and require open areas for basking in the sun. As carnivores, they eat a wide variety of prey, from fish and toads to small antelopes. They will also scavenge on carrion.

FUN FACT

Monitor lizards pick up the scent of prey using their forked tongue.

PANTHER CHAMELEON

FALL ABOUT

Panther chameleons can change color quickly. When males fight, they display dazzling hues. The male with the brightest colors usually wins the battle.

- **Length:** 16 to 21 inches (40.6 to 53.3 cm)
- **Weight:** 5 to 6.3 ounces (141.7 to 178.6 g)
- **Lifespan:** 1 to 2 years
- **Conservation Status:** Least Concern

HABITAT & DIET

Panther chameleons are omnivores, but they primarily eat insects. They live in the humid forests of Madagascar.

FUN FACT

Chameleons can search for food with one eye while the other watches for danger.

FAMILY & SOCIAL LIFE

Both males and females are solitary. They come together only to mate. Mothers abandon their eggs after laying them. Babies are completely independent from birth.

STRIPED SKINK

ALL ABOUT

Skinks are medium-sized lizards with short legs and slender bodies. The African striped skink is brownish with two stripes running down its body.

- **Length:** 7 to 10 inches (17.8 to 25.4 cm)
- **Weight:** about 7 to 9 ounces (198.4 to 255.1 g)
- **Lifespan:** 5 to 7 years
- **Conservation Status:** Least Concern

HABITAT & DIET

These skinks occupy underground burrows in grasslands and forests. They eat insects, spiders, fruit, and seeds.

FAMILY & SOCIAL LIFE

The African striped skink leads a mostly solitary life.

DID YOU KNOW?

This skink has transparent scales instead of lower eyelids, allowing the skink to see while also protecting its eyes.

SUNGAZER LIZARD

ALL ABOUT

The sungazer is the largest type of girdled lizard, a family that also includes the armadillo lizard. Thick, spiny scales cover most of its body.

- **Length:** 8 to 13.8 inches (20.3 to 35.1 cm)
- **Weight:** 6.5 to 11.3 ounces (184.3 to 320.3 g)
- **Lifespan:** up to 25 years
- **Conservation Status:** Vulnerable

HABITAT & DIET

This burrowing lizard is only found in the highlands of South Africa. It eats invertebrates, especially beetles.

FAMILY & SOCIAL LIFE

This lizard is social, living in small groups. Females give birth to live young after a pregnancy that may last up to two years.

FUN FACT

This lizard is named for its habit of lifting its head toward the sun.

BLACK MAMBA

FUN FACT

The black mamba is one of the world's fastest snakes.

ALL ABOUT

The black mamba isn't black but rather gray or olive brown. Its name comes from the dark color inside its mouth, which the black mamba will flash in warning. This highly venomous snake is known for its speed and aggressive nature.

- **Length:** 6.6 to 14 feet (2 to 4.3 m)
- **Weight:** 2 to 3.5 pounds (0.9 to 1.6 kg)
- **Lifespan:** up to 11 years
- **Conservation Status:** Least Concern

HABITAT & DIET

The black mamba inhabits savannas, woodlands, and rocky hills. It hunts small mammals and birds, which it eats whole. It can swallow prey up to four times the size of its mouth.

FAMILY & SOCIAL LIFE

Black mambas are largely solitary.

BOOMSLANG

ALL ABOUT

With a powerful venom, the boomslang is a silent hunter, gliding through trees in search of prey. A male's scales are typically light green with dark edges. Females may be darker green or brown. Boomslangs have large eyes and excellent vision.

- **Length:** 3.5 to 6.5 feet (1.1 to 2 m)
- **Weight:** 6 to 18 ounces (170.1 to 510.3 g)
- **Lifespan:** up to 6 years
- **Conservation Status:** Least Concern

HABITAT & DIET

Boomslangs spend most of their time in trees, hunting arboreal prey such as birds and lizards. They live in forested areas.

FAMILY & SOCIAL LIFE

Boomslangs are solitary. Like most snake species, females abandon eggs after they are laid. Babies are independent from birth.

DID YOU KNOW?

Boomslangs are rear-fanged venomous snakes. Rather than a single stabbing strike, rear-fanged snakes bite down on their prey for a longer time to get the venom into their victims.

DESERT HORNED VIPER

ALL ABOUT

The desert horned viper was named for the two pointy scales on its head. This venomous snake buries its body to escape the heat and to wait for prey. When prey comes near, it launches a surprise attack. Its horns are believed to provide camouflage.

- **Length:** 1.6 to 2 feet (0.5 to 0.6 m)
- **Weight:** up to 1.5 pounds (0.7 kg)
- **Lifespan:** up to 18 years
- **Conservation Status:** Least Concern

HABITAT & DIET

This desert dweller eats small animal prey.

FAMILY & SOCIAL LIFE

These snakes are solitary, coming together only to mate.

FUN FACT

A viper's fangs fold back against the roof of its mouth when not in use.

DUMERIL'S BOA

ALL ABOUT

The Dumeril's boa is a large, thick-bodied snake native to Madagascar. Like other boas, it squeezes its prey to death. Its skin pattern provides excellent camouflage among dead leaves on the forest floor. An ambush hunter, it will lie motionless until prey comes close enough to capture.

- **Length:** up to 7 feet (2.1 m)
- **Weight:** up to 20 pounds (9.1 kg)
- **Lifespan:** 20 to 30 years
- **Conservation Status:** Least Concern

DID YOU KNOW?

The Dumeril's boa is ovoviviparous, meaning its young grow in eggs, but the eggs hatch while they are still inside the mother's body.

HABITAT & DIET

This boa prefers dry forested regions. Its diverse diet includes lemurs, birds, reptiles, and amphibians.

FAMILY & SOCIAL LIFE

This snake is solitary outside of the mating season.

EGG-EATING SNAKE

ALL ABOUT

The egg-eating snake has almost no teeth but spreads its jaw wide to suck an egg into its mouth. When the egg reaches its throat, the snake pierces the egg's shell with its spiky vertebrae.

- **Length:** 2.5 to 3 feet (0.8 to 0.9 m)
- **Weight:** up to 1 pound (0.5 kg)
- **Lifespan:** up to 7 years
- **Conservation Status:** Least Concern

HABITAT & DIET

This snake lives in deserts and grasslands. It hides under logs or rocks by day and emerges at night to search for birds' nests. Since birds breed seasonally, this snake fasts for most of the year.

FAMILY & SOCIAL LIFE

Little is known about this snake's social behavior.

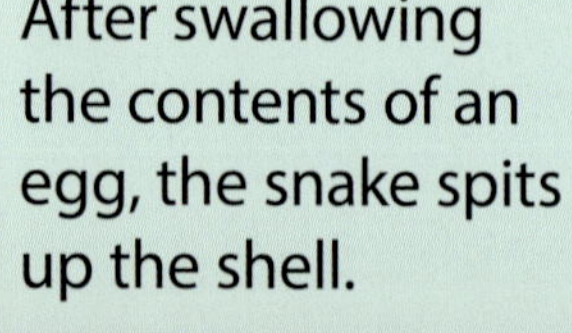

FUN FACT

After swallowing the contents of an egg, the snake spits up the shell.

GABOON VIPER

ALL ABOUT

The large, thick-bodied Gaboon viper is nearly impossible to spot when camouflaged among dead leaves on the forest floor. Its eyes are on the top of its head rather than the sides. This makes it easier for the snake to watch for prey.

- **Length:** 4 to 6.5 feet (1.2 to 2 m)
- **Weight:** up to 45 pounds (20.4 kg)
- **Lifespan:** up to 20 years
- **Conservation Status:** Vulnerable

HABITAT & DIET

This venomous snake ambushes whatever prey crosses its path, including rodents, birds, and frogs. It lives in rainforests and tropical woodlands.

FAMILY & SOCIAL LIFE

Gaboon vipers lead solitary lives. Females can give birth to 50 babies at one time.

FUN FACT

The Gaboon viper has the longest fangs of any snake.

PUFF ADDER

ALL ABOUT

The puff adder is thought to be Africa's deadliest snake. Its venom immobilizes the snake's victims immediately after a strike. The puff adder gets its name from its defense strategy. When faced with a predator, it puffs itself up to look larger.

- **Length:** 3.3 to 4.9 feet (1 to 1.5 m)
- **Weight:** 9.9 to 15 pounds (4.5 to 6.8 kg)
- **Lifespan:** up to 15 years
- **Conservation Status:** Least Concern

FUN FACT

The puff adder can suppress its scent to hide from predators and prey.

HABITAT & DIET

This terrestrial snake lives in a variety of habitat types, including grasslands and semi-deserts. It hunts at night, mostly targeting small mammals and birds.

FAMILY & SOCIAL LIFE

Outside of its once-yearly mating season, the puff adder is solitary.

ROYAL PYTHON

ALL ABOUT

Africa's smallest python, the royal python is dark brown or black with lighter blotches scattered across its body. It is also known as the ball python because it coils up in a ball if threatened. Pythons are nonvenomous snakes that kill by squeezing their prey until it can no longer breathe.

- **Length:** 3 to 6 feet (0.9 to 1.8 m)
- **Weight:** 3 to 6 pounds (1.4 to 2.7 kg)
- **Lifespan:** 10 years
- **Conservation Status:** Near Threatened

HABITAT & DIET

These ground-dwelling snakes often take refuge in burrows or in the roots of trees. They live in savannas, grasslands, and forests, where they hunt rodents and other small animals.

FAMILY & SOCIAL LIFE

Royal pythons are usually solitary.

DID YOU KNOW?

Pythons have special heat-sensing pits along their jaws that help them locate prey in the dark.

SPITTING COBRA

ALL ABOUT

Cobras are known for their ability to spread out their neck ribs, creating a hood that makes them appear larger and more threatening. Spitting cobras have grooves in their fangs that allow them to spray venom. Seven species of spitting cobra inhabit Africa. These snakes spit for defense, aiming for the eyes of an attacker.

- **Length:** 3.3 to 9 feet (1 to 2.7 m)
- **Weight:** 10 to 15.5 pounds (4.5 to 7 kg)
- **Lifespan:** up to 20 years
- **Conservation Status:** Varies by species

HABITAT & DIET

Spitting cobras inhabit savannas, deserts, and shrubland. They prey on a variety of small animals.

FAMILY & SOCIAL LIFE

These snakes are solitary.

FUN FACT

Spiral grooves in a spitting cobra's fangs improve the accuracy of its aim.

TIGER SNAKE

ALL ABOUT

The medium-sized venomous tiger snake has an orange body with dark stripes or blotches. Strictly nocturnal, it hides under rocks or trees during the day. Extra-large eyes help it see at night.

- **Length:** 1.6 to 3.3 feet (0.5 to 1 m)
- **Weight:** less than 1 pound (0.5 kg)
- **Lifespan:** up to 8 years
- **Conservation Status:** Least Concern

All snakes periodically shed their skin as they grow. A tiger snake may shed several times a year, depending on its age, size, and diet.

HABITAT & DIET

This snake is mostly found in lowland forests and savannas. It spends most of its time on the ground but is an excellent climber. Its prey includes lizards, rodents, bats, and birds.

FAMILY & SOCIAL LIFE

Like most snakes, tiger snakes come together to mate but are otherwise solitary.

ALDABRA TORTOISE

ALL ABOUT

The large Aldabra tortoise lives on a chain of islands off Africa's east coast. Its top shell, called a carapace, is thick and domed. This tortoise doesn't have teeth but rather a sharp beak. It plows a path through vegetation as it eats, creating pathways for other animals.

- **Length:** 3 to 4.5 feet (0.9 to 1.4 m)
- **Weight:** 350 to 550 pounds (158.8 to 249.5 kg)
- **Lifespan:** up to 150 years
- **Conservation Status:** Vulnerable

DID YOU KNOW?

Naturalist Charles Darwin established a breeding and conservation program for the Aldabra tortoise in the late 1800s. It was one of the first species granted such protection.

HABITAT & DIET

This tortoise lives in forests, scrublands, grasslands, and swamps. It primarily eats grasses and plants.

FAMILY & SOCIAL LIFE

These tortoises are mostly solitary but will gather around food or water sources. Hatchlings are independent from day one.

LEOPARD TORTOISE

ALL ABOUT

Dark markings on the leopard tortoise's yellowish shell somewhat resemble a leopard's spots. Like most tortoises, it can retract its head into its shell when threatened.

- **Length:** 12 to 28 inches (30.5 to 71.1 cm)
- **Weight:** 28 to 88 pounds (12.7 to 39.9 kg)
- **Lifespan:** 50 to 100 years
- **Conservation Status:** Least Concern

HABITAT & DIET

Leopard tortoises inhabit a variety of habitats. They are found from coasts to deserts and grasslands. They graze on grass, succulents, fallen fruit, and other vegetation.

FAMILY & SOCIAL LIFE

These tortoises are usually solitary.

DID YOU KNOW?

Concentric ridges on a leopard tortoise's scutes are called growth rings. Contrary to popular belief, one ring does not equal one year of life. Many factors affect the rate at which each tortoise grows.

NILE SOFTSHELL TURTLE

ALL ABOUT

The large-bodied Nile softshell turtle has a flat, rubbery shell. It is olive to brown with white spots. An excellent swimmer, it uses its webbed limbs like paddles. Tube-like nostrils allow the turtle to breathe with most of its body submerged.

- **Length:** 2.8 to 3.1 feet (0.8 to 0.9 m)
- **Weight:** 44 to 88 pounds (20 to 39.9 kg)
- **Lifespan:** 25 to 45 years
- **Conservation Status:** Vulnerable

HABITAT & DIET

This turtle lives in the Nile River and other bodies of water. It can inhabit fresh water, salt water, and brackish environments. It is mostly aquatic but will bask on shore. Its diet includes fish, crustaceans, seeds, and leaves.

FAMILY & SOCIAL LIFE

Nile softshell turtles are solitary animals.

FUN FACT

This turtle doesn't need to breathe very often. It absorbs most of its oxygen through its skin.

PANCAKE TORTOISE

FUN FACT

Pancake tortoise hatchlings aren't flat. Their rounded shells flatten as they grow.

ALL ABOUT

The pancake tortoise's carapace is thin, flat, and flexible, which allows the tortoise to squeeze into thin crevices between rocks. This species is also known for its speed. It can run fast to evade mongooses and other predators.

- **Length:** 4 to 7 inches (10.2 to 17.8 cm)
- **Weight:** 0.7 to 1.1 pounds (0.3 to 0.5 kg)
- **Lifespan:** up to 35 years
- **Conservation Status:** Critically Endangered

HABITAT & DIET

The pancake tortoise lives in dry, rocky grasslands. It eats grasses and foliage. It gets most of its water from the food that it eats.

FAMILY & SOCIAL LIFE

For a reptile, the pancake tortoise is fairly social. Pairs or even small groups will sometimes squeeze themselves into a single crevice.

ADDITIONAL REPTILES

Desert sandfish

DESERT SANDFISH

- **About:** This skink's fishy name refers to its ability to "swim" through sand.
- **Habitat:** deserts
- **Conservation Status:** Least Concern

Madagascar giant day gecko

MADAGASCAR GIANT DAY GECKO

- **About:** This day-active species is one of the world's largest geckos.
- **Habitat:** rainforests
- **Conservation Status:** Least Concern

RADIATED TORTOISE

- **About:** The radiated tortoise was named for the yellow lines radiating down the plates of its shell.
- **Habitat:** dry brush, forests, and woodlands
- **Conservation Status:** Critically Endangered

Radiated tortoise

Rhinoceros viper

RHINOCEROS VIPER

- **About:** Horn-like scales on the tip of its nose make this viper stand out.
- **Habitat:** wetlands, tropical forests
- **Conservation Status:** Vulnerable

Shovel-snouted lizard

SHOVEL-SNOUTED LIZARD

- **About:** This lizard escapes the heat by diving into sand.
- **Habitat:** desert sand dunes
- **Conservation Status:** Least Concern

Stiletto snake

STILETTO SNAKE

- **About:** Also known as the side-stabbing snake, this snake strikes by jerking its head sideways.
- **Habitat:** varied
- **Conservation Status:** Least Concern

BIRDS

At least 2,500 different bird species are found in Africa. More than half are endemic to the continent. Many species migrate at certain times of the year. Others remain in the same area year-round. Nearly all birds can fly, though Africa is home to two notable exceptions: the ostrich and the African penguin.

Birds are found throughout the African continent, with higher diversity in tropical rainforests.

Golden weaver birds make a tightly woven nest.

WHAT IS A BIRD?

- Birds are the only living animals with feathers.
- They are warm-blooded animals. Their body temperature doesn't change with the environment but remains relatively constant.
- They have wings instead of arms.
- All birds have beaks, which are also known as bills.
- Most birds' bones are hollow, an adaptation that makes them lightweight.
- Females reproduce by laying eggs.

An ostrich can run as fast as 40 miles per hour (64.4 kmh).

BIRDS

AFRICAN GRAY PARROT

ALL ABOUT

The African gray parrot is Africa's largest parrot. It has gray feathers with black wing tips and a scarlet tail. It has a black beak and bare white skin around its eyes. This species is known for its intelligence and skill at mimicry. It can have a vocabulary of several hundred words.

- **Length:** 11 to 16 inches (27.9 to 40.6 cm)
- **Weight:** 14 to 20 ounces (396.9 to 567 g)
- **Lifespan:** up to 30 years
- **Conservation Status:** Endangered

HABITAT & DIET

The African gray parrot nests in tall trees in damp forests. Its large, curved beak is designed for eating hard nuts and seeds. It also eats fruit and other vegetation.

FAMILY & SOCIAL LIFE

These birds are very social. They travel and roost in huge flocks and may break into smaller groups when feeding. They usually mate for life.

FUN FACT

African grays are popular pets.

DID YOU KNOW?

Parrots have zygodactyl feet. In this foot structure, two toes face forward and two face backward. This helps with climbing and holding food.

AFRICAN PENGUIN

ALL ABOUT

The African penguin lives along Africa's southwest coast. It is known for its donkey-like braying call, which earned it the nickname "jackass penguin." This black-and-white bird has distinct pink glands above each eye that help regulate its body temperature to cool the bird.

- **Height:** 2 to 2.3 feet (0.6 to 0.7 m)
- **Weight:** 4 to 11 pounds (1.8 to 5 kg)
- **Lifespan:** up to 11 years
- **Conservation Status:** Endangered

FUN FACT

These penguins dig their nests in layers of built-up penguin poop, also called guano.

HABITAT & DIET

African penguins spend months at sea but nest on land. Preferred habitats are rocky or sandy beaches. They mainly eat fish, especially anchovies, sardines, and mackerel.

FAMILY & SOCIAL LIFE

These highly social birds live in colonies that can range from a few dozen to more than a hundred penguins.

BATELEUR

ALL ABOUT

This colorful, medium-sized member of the eagle family has a very short tail. Bateleurs have an unusual habit of tipping side to side as they soar, like an acrobat balancing.

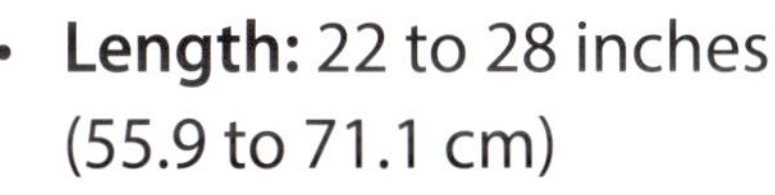

- **Length:** 22 to 28 inches (55.9 to 71.1 cm)
- **Weight:** 4 to 6.5 pounds (1.8 to 2.9 kg)
- **Lifespan:** up to 27 years
- **Conservation Status:** Endangered

HABITAT & DIET

Bateleurs prefer open woodlands and savannas. They build large nests in the forks of tall trees, which they will reuse for multiple years. They are hunters and scavengers, eating a variety of small animals and carrion.

FAMILY & SOCIAL LIFE

These birds live alone or in pairs. A pair raises its young together.

FUN FACT

These birds spend about 80 percent of their daylight hours in flight.

BEARDED BARBET

ALL ABOUT

The bearded barbet was named for the hair-like feathers that stick out under its bill. It has glossy black feathers on its back and wings, red cheeks and underparts, and a yellow patch around its eyes.

- **Length:** about 10 inches (25.4 cm)
- **Weight:** 2.8 to 3.8 ounces (79.4 to 107.7 g)
- **Lifespan:** 8 to 10 years
- **Conservation Status:** Least Concern

HABITAT & DIET

This bird lives in tropical forests. They mainly eat figs and other fruit.

FUN FACT

Barbets are related to toucans and woodpeckers.

FAMILY & SOCIAL LIFE

Barbets nest in holes in tree stumps or branches. Four or five birds may share the same tree hollow.

BUFFALO WEAVER

ALL ABOUT

Weavers are birds that weave large, often interconnected nests out of thorny twigs. They have feet adapted for perching, with three toes pointing forward and one backward. They are very noisy.

- **Length:** 7 to 10 inches (17.8 to 25.4 cm)
- **Weight:** 2 to 3 ounces (56.7 to 85 g)
- **Lifespan:** up to 20 years
- **Conservation Status:** Least Concern

DID YOU KNOW?

Other birds will move into vacated weaver bird nests rather than build their own.

HABITAT & DIET

Buffalo weavers live in dry regions and often follow buffalo herds. They feast on the insects stirred up by the buffalo. They also eat seeds and berries.

FAMILY & SOCIAL LIFE

Buffalo weavers live in colonies of varying size. All group members assist in raising young.

CAPE VULTURE

ALL ABOUT

The large Cape vulture is creamy white with dark flight feathers. Its wingspan is about 8 feet (2.4 m) wide. Its body is adapted for scavenging. Its sharp, hooked beak tears apart flesh, and its featherless head keeps the bird clean when feeding on carcasses.

- **Length:** 38 to 43 inches (96.5 to 109.2 cm)
- **Weight:** 15 to 24 pounds (6.8 to 10.9 kg)
- **Lifespan:** 15 to 25 years
- **Conservation Status:** Vulnerable

FUN FACT

Vultures are nature's clean-up crew. By eating dead animals, they prevent the spread of disease.

HABITAT & DIET

This bird lives in diverse habitats across southern Africa, including mountains and steppes. It roosts on cliffsides and dines on carrion.

FAMILY & SOCIAL LIFE

Cape vultures are social animals. They feed, bathe, and soar in groups. Both parents incubate eggs and care for chicks.

African fish eagle

FISH EAGLE

ALL ABOUT

Fish eagles are also known as sea eagles. There are two species that live in Africa: Madagascar and African.

FUN FACT

Barbs on this eagle's feet help it hold onto slippery prey.

The African fish eagle has dark brown wings, a white head and chest, and a large yellow bill. When fishing, it flies high above the water to avoid casting a shadow on the surface. Once this raptor sees a fish, it dives feet first, snatching the fish in its talons.

- **Length:** 25 to 29.5 inches (63.5 to 74.9 cm)
- **Weight:** 4.5 to 8 pounds (2 to 3.6 kg)
- **Lifespan:** 16 to 24 years
- **Conservation Status:** Least Concern to Critically Endangered

HABITAT & DIET

The fish eagle lives near large rivers, lakes, and other bodies of water. In addition to fish, the fish eagle eats frogs, birds, and small mammals. It will steal food from other predators.

FAMILY & SOCIAL LIFE

Fish eagles may be solitary or form bonded pairs.

FLAMINGO (LESSER)

ALL ABOUT

The smallest member of the flamingo family, the lesser flamingo is pale to dark pink in color. Its colors come from pigments in the algae it eats. The lesser flamingo's curved bill is dark red with a black tip. Its eyes are yellow orange.

A flamingo's feet are webbed, and its stilt-like legs are built for wading in shallow water. These birds are also strong fliers and may travel hundreds of miles in search of food.

- **Height:** 2.6 to 2.9 feet (0.8 to 0.9 m)
- **Weight:** 3.3 to 4.5 pounds (1.5 to 2 kg)
- **Lifespan:** 20 to 30 years
- **Conservation Status:** Near Threatened

HABITAT & DIET

Flamingos are typically found in mudflats, shallow lakes, and lagoons. They filter feed by dragging their bill upside-down through the water to filter out algae.

FUN FACT

Flamingo chicks are gray. It takes a few years for their feathers to turn pink.

FAMILY & SOCIAL LIFE

A lesser flamingo flock can consist of more than one million birds. They are some of the largest bird colonies on Earth.

DID YOU KNOW?

Flamingo parents leave their chicks in a large group called a creche, which is like daycare for young animals. A few adult birds stay behind to babysit.

GRAY CROWNED CRANE

ALL ABOUT

The tall, semiaquatic gray crowned crane has a long neck, long legs, and mostly gray feathers. It has a crown of stiff, golden bristles. Unlike other cranes, these birds perch in trees thanks to prehensile hind toes that allow them to grasp branches.

- **Height:** 3.3 to 4 feet (1 to 1.2 m)
- **Weight:** 6.6 to 8.8 pounds (3 to 4 kg)
- **Lifespan:** 20 years
- **Conservation Status:** Endangered

HABITAT & DIET

Crowned cranes are found in African wetlands and grasslands. They sleep in trees at night to avoid predators. These birds eat insects, seeds, small mammals, and reptiles.

FAMILY & SOCIAL LIFE

Gray crowned cranes often mate for life. Pairs perform elaborate courtship dances to cement their bond.

FUN FACT

The red inflatable sac on this bird's throat helps amplify its honking calls.

HAMERKOP

ALL ABOUT

The hamerkop sits on hippos to stalk aquatic prey.

- **Length:** up to 2 feet (0.6 m)
- **Weight:** 14.5 to 15.1 ounces (411.1 to 428.1 g)
- **Lifespan:** up to 20 years
- **Conservation Status:** Least Concern

HABITAT & DIET

They live in habitats with a water source. Pairs build large nests. They eat fish and crustaceans.

HOOPOE

ALL ABOUT

These reddish birds have black-and-white wings and tails and feathered crests.

- **Length:** 9.8 to 12.6 inches (24.9 to 32 cm)
- **Weight:** 1.6 to 3.1 ounces (45.4 to 87.9 g)
- **Lifespan:** about 10 years
- **Conservation Status:** Least Concern

HABITAT & DIET

Hoopoes nest in tree holes. They eat insects.

FAMILY & SOCIAL LIFE

These birds are often seen in groups up to 10.

KORI BUSTARD

ALL ABOUT

The ground-dwelling kori bustard is clumsy when it flies. But it spends most of its time on the ground looking for food.

- **Height:** up to 5 feet (1.5 m)
- **Weight:** 12 to 42 pounds (5.4 to 19.1 kg)
- **Lifespan:** about 20 years
- **Conservation Status:** Near Threatened

HABITAT & DIET

Kori bustards live near water sources in woodlands, grasslands, and scrublands. They eat insects, rodents, and reptiles.

FAMILY & SOCIAL LIFE

To attract a mate, a male inflates his neck up to four times its normal size. After mating, the female cares for eggs and chicks on her own.

FUN FACT

The kori bustard is the heaviest bird that can fly.

OSTRICH

ALL ABOUT

The ostrich is the world's largest bird and belongs to a group of flightless birds called ratites. The ostrich has sharp claws and powerful legs and will kick a predator to defend itself. Its neck is long and bare. Males have dark feathers, whereas females are gray.

- **Height:** 6 to 9 feet (1.8 to 2.7 m)
- **Weight:** 220 to 330 pounds (99.8 to 149.7 kg)
- **Lifespan:** 30 to 40 years
- **Conservation Status:** Least Concern

FUN FACT

Weighing about 3 pounds (1.4 kg), an ostrich egg is the largest of any bird.

HABITAT & DIET

Ostriches live in savannas and semi-deserts. They eat plants, roots, seeds, lizards, and insects.

FAMILY & SOCIAL LIFE

A male ostrich mates with multiple females, who all lay their eggs in a communal nest. Ostrich groups often travel with zebra and antelope herds.

Red-billed oxpeckers

OXPECKER

ALL ABOUT

Oxpeckers sit on zebra, buffalo, and giraffes, eating ticks and other parasites off these mammals.

FAMILY & SOCIAL LIFE

They travel in large flocks.

- **Length:** 7.5 to 9 inches (19.1 to 22.9 cm)
- **Weight:** 1.5 to 2.5 ounces (42.5 to 70.9 g)
- **Lifespan:** up to 15 years
- **Conservation Status:** Least Concern

PINK PIGEON

- **Length:** up to 15 inches (38.1 cm)
- **Weight:** up to 12 ounces (340.2 g)
- **Lifespan:** up to 18 years
- **Conservation Status:** Vulnerable

ALL ABOUT

The pink pigeon is only found on the East African island of Mauritius. Their population once dipped below 10 birds, but they are back from the brink of extinction.

HABITAT & DIET

This forest dweller eats leaves, buds, fruit, and seeds.

PYGMY FALCON

ALL ABOUT

The pygmy falcon is Africa's smallest bird of prey. It hunts in the morning and evening to avoid the hottest parts of the day, using its keen vision to scout for prey from a high perch. Once it spots its target, it descends in a burst of speed.

- **Length:** 8 inches (20.3 cm)
- **Weight:** 2 to 3 ounces (56.7 to 85 g)
- **Lifespan:** 6 to 8 years
- **Conservation Status:** Least Concern

HABITAT & DIET

These falcons prefer dry savannas and semi-deserts with scattered trees. They roost in nests built by other birds, usually weaver birds. They mostly eat lizards, rodents, and large invertebrates.

FAMILY & SOCIAL LIFE

These falcons live singly, in pairs, or in small family groups.

FUN FACT

Pygmy falcons often bob up and down before swooping in for a kill.

SACRED IBIS

ALL ABOUT

Ibises are medium-sized wading birds with long, downward-curving bills. The sacred ibis has mostly white feathers with black wingtips and tail. Its head and neck are bare and gray black. This bird is generally quiet but occasionally makes yelping vocalizations.

- **Length:** 25.6 to 35 inches (65 to 88.9 cm)
- **Weight:** 3 to 3.3 pounds (1.4 to 1.5 kg)
- **Lifespan:** up to 25 years
- **Conservation Status:** Least Concern

FUN FACT

The sacred ibis was worshipped by ancient Egyptians.

HABITAT & DIET

These birds inhabit marshes, beaches, and grasslands. They prey upon fish, amphibians, and invertebrates but will also eat carrion.

FAMILY & SOCIAL LIFE

Ibises nest in colonies, usually in trees but sometimes on the ground amid heavy vegetation.

SECRETARY BIRD

ALL ABOUT

The long-legged secretary bird is a fearless hunter. It marches through grass, searching for prey such as venomous snakes. When it finds a victim, the secretary bird stomps on it with enough force to kill or stun it. Scales on its legs protect against snake bites.

- **Height:** 4.1 to 4.9 feet (1.2 to 1.5 m)
- **Weight:** 5 to 9.8 pounds (2.3 to 4.4 kg)
- **Lifespan:** 10 to 15 years
- **Conservation Status:** Endangered

HABITAT & DIET

The secretary bird preys on snakes, lizards, amphibians, and smaller mammals and birds. It inhabits savannas, grasslands, and semi-deserts.

FAMILY & SOCIAL LIFE

Secretary birds form lifelong pair bonds.

FUN FACT

This bird swallows snakes whole.

SHOEBILL

ALL ABOUT

Once considered part of the stork family, the shoebill is more closely related to pelicans and herons. Its name comes from its long, shoe-shaped bill, which has serrated edges and a hooked tip for stabbing prey.

- **Height:** 3.5 to 5 feet (1.1 to 1.5 m)
- **Weight:** 11 to 12 pounds (5 to 5.4 kg)
- **Lifespan:** 35 years
- **Conservation Status:** Vulnerable

HABITAT & DIET

This bird inhabits wetlands. It eats large fish such as lungfish. It also eats small reptiles and amphibians. It hunts by collapsing on prey with its mouth open.

FAMILY & SOCIAL LIFE

Shoebills live alone. They are rarely seen in groups.

FUN FACT

While stalking prey, a shoebill can stand still for hours at a time.

SPOONBILL

ALL ABOUT

The mostly white spoonbill is a wading bird. It uses its spoon-shaped bill to sift through muddy water for food. Its legs are long and bright pink. It has a 4-foot (1.2 m) wingspan.

- **Height:** 2.5 to 3 feet (0.8 to 0.9 m)
- **Weight:** 3 to 4.5 pounds (1.4 to 2 kg)
- **Lifespan:** 15 years
- **Conservation Status:** Least Concern

DID YOU KNOW?

What appear to be a spoonbill's knees are actually its ankles. Birds' knees are higher up and often hidden by their feathers.

HABITAT & DIET

Spoonbills roost in trees or reeds near lakes, marshes, and other bodies of water. They eat a variety of aquatic creatures.

FAMILY & SOCIAL LIFE

Spoonbills gather in large groups during the breeding season. The rest of the year, they live alone or in small groups.

ADDITIONAL BIRDS

BEE-EATER

- **About:** Bee-eaters catch bees and other flying insects in midair.
- **Habitat:** savannas, desert steppe, open scrub
- **Conservation Status:** Least Concern

Bee-eater

Egyptian goose

EGYPTIAN GOOSE

- **About:** Ancient Egyptians considered these birds sacred.
- **Habitat:** wetlands, grasslands
- **Conservation Status:** Least Concern

Go-away bird

GO-AWAY BIRD

- **About:** This noisy bird's call sounds like "G'way!"
- **Habitat:** forests, woodlands, savannas
- **Conservation Status:** Least Concern

Malachite kingfisher

Marabou stork

MALACHITE KINGFISHER

- **About:** This diving bird has vivid orange-and-blue plumage.
- **Habitat:** near water in a variety of habitats
- **Conservation Status:** Least Concern

MARABOU STORK

- **About:** This bizarre-looking bird stands as tall as a person.
- **Habitat:** savannas, aquatic regions
- **Conservation Status:** Least Concern

ROSE-RINGED PARAKEET

- **About:** Males of this species have a pink-and-black ring around their neck.
- **Habitat:** grasslands, wetlands, forests
- **Conservation Status:** Least Concern

Rose-ringed parakeet

FISH

Fish are generally divided into two categories based on their skeleton type. Most fish are bony fish. Their skeletons are made of bone. Sharks, rays, and skates are cartilaginous fish. They have cartilage in place of bones.

Fish are found throughout the African continent, in lakes, streams, marshes, and ponds. They are also found along the coasts, in offshore reefs, and in the open sea. Like birds, some fish species migrate long distances.

WHAT IS A FISH?

Humphead cichlids live in Africa's Lake Tanganyika.

- Fish are aquatic animals. Some live in fresh water, some live in salt water, and a few can survive in either.
- They are vertebrates with backbones.
- They are cold-blooded animals. Their body temperature comes from the surrounding water.
- All fish have gills, which extract oxygen from water. The West African lungfish also has lungs.
- Fish have fins that they use for balance and movement.
- Most fish have scales.

Great white sharks hunt for Cape fur seals along the coast of South Africa.

ATLANTIC MUDSKIPPER

ALL ABOUT

Mudskippers are amphibious fish, splitting their time between land and water. Their pectoral fins function like legs, allowing them to pull themselves out of the water. They have gills but can also breathe through their skin. Frog-like eyes on the top of the mudskipper's head provide a wide range of vision.

- **Length:** 2.8 to 6 inches (7.1 to 15.2 cm)
- **Weight:** 0.3 to 2.3 ounces (8.5 to 65.2 g)
- **Lifespan:** up to 5 years
- **Conservation Status:** Least Concern

HABITAT & DIET

These fish are found in swampy, muddy areas along the West African coastline. They eat worms, insects, fish, and crustaceans.

FAMILY & SOCIAL LIFE

Male mudskippers dig deep tunnels in mud in which females lay eggs.

FUN FACT

These fish can walk on land.

CUCKOO CATFISH

ALL ABOUT

The cuckoo catfish is a brood parasite. It tricks another fish, the cichlid, into raising its young.

- **Length:** 6 to 10 inches (15.2 to 25.4 cm)
- **Weight:** less than 14 ounces (396.9 g)
- **Lifespan:** up to 15 years
- **Conservation Status:** Least Concern

HABITAT & DIET

This fish is only found in Lake Tanganyika, Tanzania, where it lives and feeds at the muddy lake bottom.

ELEPHANTNOSE FISH

ALL ABOUT

The trunk-like protrusion on this elephantnose fish's head is like a sensory rod, used for detecting prey and navigating its environment.

- **Length:** 9 to 13 inches (22.9 to 33 cm)
- **Weight:** less than 1 pound (0.5 kg)
- **Lifespan:** 6 to 10 years
- **Conservation Status:** Least Concern

HABITAT & DIET

This fish prefers slow-moving rivers. It feeds at night on worms and insects.

GREAT WHITE SHARK

ALL ABOUT

The world's largest predatory fish, the great white shark has up to 300 sharp, serrated teeth, which are replaced throughout the shark's lifetime. Great whites go on long migrations in search of food. These aggressive hunters have strong senses that help them locate prey.

- **Length:** 12 to 21 feet (3.7 to 6.4 m)
- **Weight:** 1,500 to 4,000 pounds (680.4 to 1,814.4 kg)
- **Lifespan:** up to 70 years
- **Conservation Status:** Vulnerable

FUN FACT

Newborn great white pups are more than 5 feet (1.5 m) long.

HABITAT & DIET

Found in oceans around the world, great white sharks live in large numbers off the coast of South Africa, where food is abundant. They eat seals, sea lions, sea turtles, and other marine mammals.

FAMILY & SOCIAL LIFE

These sharks are mostly solitary. Pups are independent from birth.

MALAWI CICHLID

ALL ABOUT

There are more than 1,000 species of cichlids. Most are found only in Lake Malawi.

- **Length:** 1 to 9 inches (2.5 to 22.9 cm)
- **Weight:** up to 0.3 pounds (0.1 kg)
- **Lifespan:** up to 12 years
- **Conservation Status:** Varies by species

FAMILY & SOCIAL LIFE

Females choose mates based on a male's characteristics, usually color or pattern.

ORNATE BICHIR

ALL ABOUT

The ornate bichir has a row of spiny fins along its back. Gills and a blowhole allow this fish to spend time out of water.

- **Length:** 16 to 24 inches (40.6 to 61 cm)
- **Weight:** up to 18 ounces (510.3 g)
- **Lifespan:** 10 to 15 years
- **Conservation Status:** Least Concern

HABITAT & DIET

Bichir are native to streams and rivers in the Congo Basin. They mainly eat fish and worms.

PYJAMA SHARK

ALL ABOUT

The pyjama shark belongs to the catshark family, named for their cat-like eyes. Pyjama sharks have dark, parallel stripes. They only live off the coast of southern Africa.

- **Length:** 2 to 3.3 feet (0.6 to 1 m)
- **Weight:** 15 to 17 pounds (6.8 to 7.7 kg)
- **Lifespan:** up to 21 years
- **Conservation Status:** Least Concern

DID YOU KNOW?

Barbels, the fleshy projections on this shark's nose, are used to help locate prey.

HABITAT & DIET

Pyjama sharks live on the ocean floor, resting by day in caves or kelp beds. At night, these nocturnal sharks hunt for small fish and crustaceans.

FAMILY & SOCIAL LIFE

These sharks are usually seen alone or in pairs. Like many sharks, pyjama shark females lay their eggs in a thick, protective case, known as a mermaid's purse.

TIGERFISH

ALL ABOUT

Like a tiger, the tigerfish not only has stripes, but it is also a fierce predator. It uses its dagger-like teeth to chomp on smaller fish.

- **Length:** up to 6 feet (1.8 m)
- **Weight:** up to 125 pounds (56.7 kg)
- **Lifespan:** up to 10 years
- **Conservation Status:** Least Concern

HABITAT & DIET

Tigerfish rest at the bottom of rivers and lakes and move closer to the surface during the day. They mainly hunt fish but will also eat insects and birds.

FAMILY & SOCIAL LIFE

A male creates a circular nest in the sand and then attracts a mate with his colorful fins. The female lays up to 20,000 eggs at once. The male guards the eggs until they hatch.

FUN FACT

Tigerfish have been seen leaping out of the water to catch birds in flight.

ADDITIONAL FISH

African butterflyfish

AFRICAN BUTTERFLYFISH

- **About:** The butterflyfish can leap out of the water to catch insects.
- **Habitat:** swamps, rivers, and ponds
- **Conservation Status:** Least Concern

Blue-spotted stingray

BLUE-SPOTTED STINGRAY

- **About:** This stingray has bright blue spots and venomous spines on its tail.
- **Habitat:** sandy sea bottoms, primarily near coral reefs
- **Conservation Status:** Least Concern

COELACANTH

- **About:** This ancient fish species has been around since before dinosaurs roamed the earth.
- **Habitat:** deep waters off the eastern coast of Africa
- **Conservation Status:** Critically Endangered

Coelacanth

KNYSNA SEAHORSE

- **About:** This South African species is the world's most endangered seahorse.
- **Habitat:** estuaries and lagoons
- **Conservation Status:** Endangered

Knysna seahorse

MBU PUFFERFISH

- **About:** When threatened, pufferfish gulp water to inflate their body.
- **Habitat:** freshwater rivers, lakes, and estuaries
- **Conservation Status:** Least Concern

WEST AFRICAN LUNGFISH

- **About:** In a drought, lungfish burrow into mud and go dormant.
- **Habitat:** freshwater lakes, rivers, and wetlands
- **Conservation Status:** Least Concern

West African lungfish

Mbu pufferfish

AMPHIBIANS

The word *amphibian* means "double life." Most amphibians spend their early days in water and their adulthood on land. This class of animals includes frogs, toads, salamanders, newts, and caecilians.

The majority of amphibians in Africa are frogs and toads. Salamanders and newts are very rare. Most amphibians live in warm climates near water. Some can survive in colder or hotter regions. Rain frogs, for example, have adapted to live in dry African deserts. They hibernate underground until heavy rains come.

WHAT IS AN AMPHIBIAN?

- Amphibians have moist skin.
- Their skin is permeable. It can absorb water.
- They don't have hair, feathers, or scales.
- Most amphibians can breathe through both their lungs and skin.
- They are cold-blooded. They cannot produce their own body heat.
- Most go through a three-stage life cycle: egg to larvae to adult.

In dry conditions, the giant African bullfrog may form a cocoon to keep it from drying out.

Painted reed frogs may differ in color between the day and night.

AFRICAN CLAWED FROG

ALL ABOUT

The bottom-dwelling African clawed frog has clawed toes on its hind feet and long, unwebbed fingers on its front feet. Unlike most frogs, it doesn't have a tongue with which to catch food. It uses fingers to scoop food into its mouth.

- **Length:** 2.2 to 4.7 inches (5.6 to 11.9 cm)
- **Weight:** 2 to 7 ounces (56.7 to 198.4 g)
- **Lifespan:** up to 15 years
- **Conservation Status:** Least Concern

HABITAT & DIET

This frog will eat a variety of living and dead organic matter. Mostly aquatic, it prefers warm, stagnant lakes and ponds.

FUN FACT

These frogs can swim quickly in any direction, even backward.

FAMILY & SOCIAL LIFE

Males are much smaller than females. A female can lay up to 2,000 eggs in a night. The eggs hatch about a week later.

BUSHVELD RAIN FROG

ALL ABOUT

The Bushveld rain frog spends most of its time in underground burrows, emerging to look for food or mates.

- **Length:** 1.2 to 2.3 inches (3 to 5.8 cm)
- **Weight:** less than 1 ounce (28.3 g)
- **Lifespan:** up to 15 years
- **Conservation Status:** Least Concern

FAMILY & SOCIAL LIFE

These frogs only mate after a heavy rainfall. The young frogs hatch as froglets, skipping the tadpole phase altogether.

FIRE SALAMANDER

ALL ABOUT

The fire salamander has bright yellow spots to warn predators it is toxic. It also has glands behind its eyes that can spray poison.

- **Length:** 5 to 12 inches (12.7 to 30.5 cm)
- **Weight:** less than 1 ounce (28.3 g)
- **Lifespan:** up to 14 years
- **Conservation Status:** Vulnerable

HABITAT & DIET

It lives on the floor of mountain forests. It hides under leaf litter, logs, or stones.

GOLIATH BULLFROG

ALL ABOUT

The goliath bullfrog is the world's largest frog. This frog's slick skin earned it the nickname "giant slippery frog." Males are significantly larger and stronger than females.

- **Length:** 4 to 13 inches (10.2 to 33 cm)
- **Weight:** 1.3 to 7.2 pounds (0.6 to 3.3 kg)
- **Lifespan:** up to 15 years
- **Conservation Status:** Endangered

HABITAT & DIET

Goliath bullfrogs live in rainforest streams and ponds. An excellent swimmer, it rarely emerges onto land. Its diet includes fish, insects, and other amphibians.

FAMILY & SOCIAL LIFE

Males wrestle to compete for females. They build rocky nests in which the female deposits her eggs.

FUN FACT

This frog doesn't croak. It lacks a vocal sac.

GUTTURAL TOAD

ALL ABOUT

The guttural toad thrives in southern Africa's warm, humid climate. Males have vocal sacs that inflate like balloons. Vocal sacs amplify sound and are used to lure mates.

- **Length:** 2.5 to 4.7 inches (6.4 to 11.9 cm)
- **Weight:** 0.7 to 1.4 ounces (19.8 to 39.7 g)
- **Lifespan:** up to 7 years
- **Conservation Status:** Least Concern

FUN FACT

Toads can live in drier places than frogs.

HABITAT & DIET

These toads live in a variety of habitats, including pastures and urban areas. They mostly eat insects but will also consume lizards and amphibians.

FAMILY & SOCIAL LIFE

Females are attracted by the males' calls, which sound like loud snores. Females lay eggs in long, double strings, which they wrap around rocks or vegetation.

LEAF-FOLDING FROG

ALL ABOUT

After a leaf-folding frog lays her eggs on a leaf, she folds the leaf around them, fastening it with a sticky secretion. This makeshift envelope protects the eggs while they develop.

- **Length:** 1.2 to 1.5 inches (3 to 3.8 cm)
- **Weight:** less than 1 ounce (28.3 g)
- **Lifespan:** up to 5 years
- **Conservation Status:** Least Concern

FUN FACT

These frogs are often called banana frogs.

HABITAT & DIET

Leaf-folding frogs live near densely vegetated streams and swamps. They eat small invertebrates.

FAMILY & SOCIAL LIFE

Males make rapid clicking sounds to attract females. A female may mate with multiple males. Outside of breeding, these frogs are typically solitary.

MANTELLA FROG

ALL ABOUT

Mantellas have brightly colored skin and toxic secretions. These Madagascar natives display a wide range of colors.

- **Length:** 0.7 to 2 inches (1.8 to 5.1 cm)
- **Weight:** up to 2 ounces (56.7 g)
- **Lifespan:** up to 8 years
- **Conservation Status:** Varies by species

HABITAT & DIET

Mantellas get their toxins from their diet of primarily ants, termites, and fruit flies. They are mostly terrestrial, but some spend time in trees.

PAINTED REED FROG

ALL ABOUT

Painted reed frogs have adhesive pads on their toes to help them climb and cling to foliage. They rest on leaves and can remain still for hours.

- **Length:** 1.3 to 1.7 inches (3.3 to 4.3 cm)
- **Weight:** up to 1 ounce (28.3 g)
- **Lifespan:** 3 to 5 years
- **Conservation Status:** Least Concern

HABITAT & DIET

These frogs prefer densely vegetated wetlands. They eat insects.

ADDITIONAL AMPHIBIANS

Algerian ribbed newt

ALGERIAN RIBBED NEWT

- **About:** A ribbed newt can poke its pointy ribs through its skin to stab an attacker.
- **Habitat:** rivers, swamps, and marshlands
- **Conservation Status:** Least Concern

Hairy frog

HAIRY FROG

- **About:** Hair-like skin on this frog's hips helps it absorb extra oxygen.
- **Habitat:** moist forests and wetlands
- **Conservation Status:** Least Concern

SAHARA FROG

- **About:** This large frog can live in arid deserts as long as water is present.
- **Habitat:** North African wetlands
- **Conservation Status:** Least Concern

Sahara frog

Tomato frog

TOMATO FROG

- **About:** Females of this poisonous species are bright red.
- **Habitat:** forests and wetlands on the northeastern coast of Madagascar
- **Conservation Status:** Least Concern

West African live-bearing toad

WEST AFRICAN LIVE-BEARING TOAD

- **About:** This rare toad gives birth to live young.
- **Habitat:** high-altitude grasslands
- **Conservation Status:** Critically Endangered

Western leopard toad

WESTERN LEOPARD TOAD

- **About:** This South African species is named for its spotted pattern.
- **Habitat:** lakes, swamps, and ponds
- **Conservation Status:** Endangered

INVERTEBRATES

There are more invertebrates on Earth than any other type of animal. At least 90 percent of all living species belong to this group. They range in size from microscopic mites to giant squids. They come in a wide array of shapes. Some have soft bodies, whereas others have a protective outer shell called an exoskeleton.

The largest group are the insects, which include beetles, ants, moths, and butterflies. Other invertebrate categories include mollusks (such as clams and snails), arachnids (spiders and scorpions), and echinoderms (like starfish and sea urchins).

Invertebrates inhabit every type of habitat in Africa, but they are most plentiful in oceans. It is difficult to estimate the number of invertebrates on this continent because new species are discovered every year.

WHAT IS AN INVERTEBRATE?

- They don't have a backbone.
- They are cold-blooded.

King baboon spiders live in the savannas of East Africa.

Mother-of-pearl butterflies live in the forests of Africa.

Emperor scorpions are one of the largest scorpions in the world.

COMET MOTH

ALL ABOUT

The bright yellow comet moth is one of the largest moths in the world. It was named for its long red-and-yellow tail, which looks like a comet's trail.

- **Length:** 8 to 12 inches (20.3 to 30.5 cm)
- **Weight:** less than 1 ounce (28.3 g)
- **Lifespan:** up to 1 week
- **Conservation Status:** Not Assessed

HABITAT & DIET

Comet moths live in the rainforests of Madagascar. As caterpillars, they feed on leaves. Once they transform into moths, they do not eat. As a result, they only survive for about a week after emerging from their cocoons. Like most moths, they only fly at night.

FAMILY & SOCIAL LIFE

Males use their feathery antennae to detect females.

DID YOU KNOW?

Like many prey species, the comet moth has eyespots that may scare or confuse predators.

FUN FACT

Moths and butterflies are the adult form of caterpillars.

DUNG BEETLE

ALL ABOUT

By eating and burying the dung of other animals, dung beetles keep ecosystems healthy. Scientists divide dung beetle species into three basic types: rollers, tunnelers, and dwellers. Rollers form dung into balls and roll them away before burying them. Tunnelers burrow under dung. Dwellers live inside dung piles.

- **Length:** up to 2.5 inches (6.4 cm)
- **Weight:** up to 3.5 ounces (99.2 g)
- **Lifespan:** 3 years
- **Conservation Status:** Data Deficient

HABITAT & DIET

Dung beetles live in deserts, grasslands, and rainforests. They primarily eat animal feces, but some also consume fungi, fruit, and decaying plants.

FAMILY & SOCIAL LIFE

Females lay their eggs in dung. When larvae hatch, they eat dung too.

DID YOU KNOW?

Some dung beetles use starlight to navigate. They are the first insect known to do so.

EMPEROR SCORPION

ALL ABOUT

Emperor scorpions live in small groups. They have a pair of pincers and a stinger.

- **Length:** up to 8 inches (20.3 cm)
- **Weight:** up to 1.5 ounces (42.5 g)
- **Lifespan:** 6 to 8 years
- **Conservation Status:** Not Assessed

HABITAT & DIET

Emperor scorpions live in humid habitats. They eat insects and small vertebrates.

KING BABOON SPIDER

ALL ABOUT

A king baboon spider lifts its front limbs and displays its fangs. It also creates a hissing sound with its front legs.

- **Length:** up to 8 inches (20.3 cm)
- **Weight:** up to 3 ounces (85 g)
- **Lifespan:** up to 20 years
- **Conservation Status:** Not Assessed

MADAGASCAR HISSING COCKROACH

ALL ABOUT

The Madagascar hissing cockroach is the only cockroach that can hiss. It does so by expelling air through spiracles, which are tiny holes in its sides. Hissing plays a part in mating and defense.

- **Length:** 2 to 3 inches (5.1 to 7.6 cm)
- **Weight:** 0.2 to 0.8 ounces (5.7 to 22.7 g)
- **Lifespan:** 2 to 5 years
- **Conservation Status:** Not Assessed

FUN FACT

Madagascar hissing cockroaches are commonly kept as pets.

HABITAT & DIET

Hissing cockroaches inhabit leaf litter, rotting logs, and other debris. They are detritivores, meaning they eat dead and decaying organisms.

FAMILY & SOCIAL LIFE

These social insects live in large colonies. Males will fight over females. The male that hisses the most usually wins.

RAINBOW LOCUST

ALL ABOUT

Bright colors warn predators that the rainbow locust has toxins, which come from its diet. When disturbed, the locust produces a disagreeable odor.

- **Length:** up to 3.9 inches (9.9 cm)
- **Weight:** up to 1 ounce (28.3 g)
- **Lifespan:** up to 8 months
- **Conservation Status:** Not Assessed

HABITAT & DIET

These locusts live in grasslands, shrublands, and forests. They eat milkweed and toxic plants.

RHINOCEROS BEETLE

ALL ABOUT

Males use their long horns to battle for mates. Females are smaller than males and have no horns.

- **Length:** up to 6 inches (15.2 cm)
- **Weight:** up to 1 ounce (28.3 g)
- **Lifespan:** 1 to 2 years
- **Conservation Status:** Not Assessed

HABITAT & DIET

Rhinoceros beetles are found in rainforests. They eat plant material.

VELVET WORM

ALL ABOUT

Unlike earthworms, velvet worms have legs, and lots of them. Glands on the sides of their mouth produce a sticky slime. To capture prey, the velvet worm shoots this slime at high force, forming a kind of instantaneous net.

- **Length:** 0.6 to 6 inches (1.5 to 15.2 cm)
- **Weight:** less than 1 ounce (28.3 g)
- **Lifespan:** about 5 years
- **Conservation Status:** Varies by species

HABITAT & DIET

Velvet worms are sensitive to light and spend the daylight hours hiding in dark, damp places. They are often found under debris on the forest floor. They dine on insects and other invertebrates.

FAMILY & SOCIAL LIFE

These worms are generally solitary.

FUN FACT

A velvet worm can have 14 to 43 pairs of legs.

ADDITIONAL INVERTEBRATES

African giant snail

AFRICAN GIANT SNAIL

- **About:** This cone-shaped snail can grow to more than 8 inches (20.3 cm) long.
- **Habitat:** forests
- **Diet:** plants, fruit

BOMBARDIER BEETLE

- **About:** The bombardier beetle blasts boiling chemicals out of its backside to defend itself against predators.
- **Habitat:** woodlands, grasslands
- **Diet:** small insects

Bombardier beetle

Camel spider

CAMEL SPIDER

- **About:** This arachnid is known for its oversized jaws.
- **Habitat:** deserts
- **Diet:** termites, beetles, rodents, lizards, and small birds

DEATH'S-HEAD HAWKMOTH

- **About:** This moth gets its name from the skull-like pattern on its back.
- **Habitat:** various dry, warm habitats
- **Diet:** nectar and honey

GLADIATOR BUG

- **About:** These long, wingless insects are carnivorous predators.
- **Habitat:** deserts, mountains
- **Diet:** insects

MOTHER-OF-PEARL BUTTERFLY

- **About:** The wings of this iridescent butterfly are covered in scales that reflect light.
- **Habitat:** forests
- **Diet:** nectar of flowering plants

Mother-of-pearl butterfly

Gladiator bug

Death's-head hawkmoth

GLOSSARY

adaptation
A behavior or trait that helps an animal survive.

amplify
To make louder.

arboreal
Living mostly in trees.

arid
Very dry; having little or no rain.

biped
An animal that uses two legs to walk.

carrion
Dead and decaying flesh.

ecosystem
A community of all the living things in an area.

endangered
At risk of extinction.

forage
To wander in search of food.

inhabit
To live in a place.

keystone species
A species that has an especially large impact on its ecosystem.

nocturnal
Mostly active at night.

pinniped
A marine mammal with flippers that enable it to walk on land.

prehensile
Able to grasp.

regurgitate
To bring swallowed food back up into the mouth.

scavenger
An animal that mostly eats animals that it did not kill.

scute
A bony plate on the shell of a turtle or tortoise.

symbiotic
A relationship between two animals that depend on each other.

terrestrial
Living mostly or entirely on the ground.

TO LEARN MORE

FURTHER READINGS

Burnie, David. *The Animal Book: A Visual Encyclopedia of Life on Earth*. DK Children, 2013.

Drimmer, Stephanie Warren. *Roar! 100 Fun Facts About African Animals*. National Geographic, 2018.

Joubert, Dereck and Beverly. *The Ultimate Book of African Animals*. National Geographic, 2021.

Orr, Tamra B. *Awesome Animals of Africa: The Continent and Its Creatures Great and Small*. Curious Fox Books, 2024.

Vanden Branden, Claire. *Africa*. Cody Koala, 2018.

ONLINE RESOURCES

To learn more about African animals, please visit **abdobooklinks.com** or scan this QR code. These links are routinely monitored and updated to provide the most current information available.

INDEX

PHOTO CREDITS

Cover Photos: Eric Isselee/Shutterstock, front (Jackson's chameleon), front (cheetah), front (mandrill), back (ring-tailed lemur); Richard Peterson/Shutterstock, front (elephant); LouisLotterPhotography/Shutterstock, front (flamingo); FrentaN/Shutterstock, front (giraffe); photomaster/Shutterstock, front (rainbow locust); Zakir61/Shutterstock, front (lion); Aedka Studio/Shutterstock, front (rhinoceros beetle); Patryk Kosmider/Shutterstock, front (zebra); milart/Shutterstock, back (fire salamander); Roman Samokhin/Shutterstock, back (gorilla)
Interior Photos: LouisLotterPhotography/Shutterstock, 1, 145; Sam DCruz/Shutterstock, 4; Angelo Cavalli/Stone/Getty Images, 5; Designua/Shutterstock, 6; Martin Harvey/The Image Bank/Getty Images, 7, 90, 154; Seyms Brugger/Shutterstock, 8; KenCanning/E+/Getty Images, 9 (top); Dietmar Rauscher/Shutterstock, 9 (bottom); Max Allen/Shutterstock, 10; Chen Cheng/Xinhua News Agency/Getty Images, 11; imageBROKER/Frank Schneider/Getty Images, 12; McPHOTO/picture alliance/blickwinkel/M/Newscom, 13; Mateo Juric/Shutterstock, 14; Roger de la Harpe/Education Images/Universal Images Group/Getty Images, 15; Werner LAYER/Gamma-Rapho/Getty Images, 16; Eric Lafforgue/Art in All of Us/Corbis News/Getty Images, 17, 21, 58; Edwin Remsburg/VW Pics/Universal Images Group/Getty Images, 18–19; Roger de la Harpe/Shutterstock, 22; Education Images/Universal Images Group/Getty Images, 23 (top); Eric Isselee/Shutterstock, 23 (bottom), 29, 31, 51 (bottom), 86, 112 (top), 123 (top); Claire Fulton/Dreamstime, 24; Ondrej Prosicky/Shutterstock, 25, 141;Alamin-Khan/Shutterstock, 26; Michal Ninger/Shutterstock, 27; Cameron Spencer/Getty Images News/Getty Images, 28; Jami Tarris/Stone/Getty Images, 30, 108; slowmotiongli/iStock/Getty Images, 32, 166 (top), 166 (bottom); Howard Klaaste/Shutterstock, 33; Matthew P. Wicks/Moment Open/Getty Images, 34; Reynold Mainse/Design Pics/Getty Images, 35; diegograndi/iStock/Getty Images, 36 (left); RicciPhotos/iStock/Getty Images, 36 (right); cherokeejones/iStock/Getty Images, 37; Vicki Jauron, Babylon and Beyond Photography/Moment/Getty Images, 38–39, 48 (bottom); Cheryl Bronson/Moment/Getty Images, 40; Tier Und Naturfotografie J und C Sohns/Photodisc/Getty Images, 41 (top); Beate Wolter/Shutterstock, 41 (bottom); Jose_Gonzalez_Jr/iStock/Getty Images, 42; McDonald Wildlife Photography Inc./The Image Bank/Getty Images, 43, 71, 82; VisionsofAmerica/Joe Sohm/DigitalVision/Getty Images, 45; Image Source/Connect Images/Getty Images, 46; Danny Ye/Shutterstock, 47; Manoj Shah/Stone/Getty Images, 48 (top), 155; Hyserb/Shutterstock, 49; wrangel/iStock/Getty Images, 50; Mark Newman/The Image Bank/Getty Images, 51 (top); Kevin Schafer/The Image Bank/Getty Images, 52; anankkml/iStock/Getty Images, 53; Iv-olga/Shutterstock, 54; EcoPic/iStock/Getty Images, 55; Anup Shah/DigitalVision/Getty Images, 56; Robert Harding Video/Shutterstock, 57; Digital Vision/Getty Images, 59; Tom Applegate/Moment/Getty Images, 60; javarman/Shutterstock, 61; John Knight/Moment/Getty Images, 62; Anup Shah/Stone/Getty Images, 63, 70, 80 (top); USO/iStock/Getty Images, 65; Dennis Jacobsen/Shutterstock, 66 (top); Jukka Jantunen/Shutterstock, 66 (bottom); Dane Jorgensen/Shutterstock, 67; RudiHulshof/iStock/Getty Images, 68; Henk Bogaard/iStock/Getty Images, 69; IJdema/iStock/Getty Images, 72; Artush/Shutterstock, 73, 184 (top); mbrand85/Shutterstock, 74; Edwin Butter/Shutterstock, 75; alukich/iStock/Getty Images, 76; slowmotiongli/Shutterstock, 77, 132 (bottom), 161 (bottom); ChGR/E+/Getty Images, 79; Ryan M. Bolton/Shutterstock, 80 (bottom); David Schenfeld/500px Prime/Getty Images, 81; Passakorn Umpornmaha/Shutterstock, 83; Dmitri Zelenevski/iStock/Getty Images, 84; Yerbolat Shadrakhov/Shutterstock, 85 (top); Tanto Yensen/iStock/Getty Images, 85 (bottom); GlobalP/iStock/Getty Images, 86–87; Farinosa/iStock/Getty Images, 88; EcoPrint/Shutterstock, 89, 106–107, 124 (bottom), 173; Vladislav T. Jirousek/Shutterstock, 91, 105 (bottom left); phototrip/iStock/Getty Images, 92; Manuel ROMARIS/Moment/Getty Images, 93; thierry_aebischer_chinko/iNaturalist, 94; Meoita/Shutterstock, 95; Winfried Wisniewski/The Image Bank/Getty Images, 96; Francois6/iStock/Getty Images, 97; all images copyright of Jamie Lamb - elusive-images.co.uk/Moment/Getty Images, 99; Thomas Torget/Shutterstock, 100; 2630ben/iStock/Getty Images, 101; Henrik Karlsson/Moment/Getty Images, 102 (top), 102 (bottom); Gabrielle Therin-Weise/Photographer's Choice RF/Getty Images, 103; Ocean Eloy/Shutterstock, 104 (top); Kristian Bell/Moment Open/Getty Images, 104 (middle), 104 (bottom); Gerrit_de_Vries/iStock/Getty Images, 105 (top); Alan Tunnicliffe Photography/Moment/Getty Images, 105 (bottom right); Bigc Studio/Shutterstock, 107; Charlotte Bleijenberg/Shutterstock, 109; Albert Marieges/500px/500Px Plus/Getty Images, 110; NickEvansKZN/Shutterstock, 111; Jan Bures/Shutterstock, 112 (bottom); Valt Ahyppo/Shutterstock, 113; Jasius/Moment/Getty Images, 114; Freder/E+/Getty Images, 115; David Havel/Shutterstock, 116; Gaschwald/Shutterstock, 117; suebg1 photography/Moment/Getty Images, 118; Tahmid Hasan Sobuj/Shutterstock, 119, 126; Lauren Suryanata/Shutterstock, 120; Nynke van Holten/Shutterstock, 121; Matthijs Kuijpers/Dreamstime, 122; Frank Schneidermeyer/Photodisc/Getty Images, 123; fivespots/Shutterstock, 124 (top); Alan Tunnicliffe/Shutterstock, 125; reptiles4all/Shutterstock, 127 (top); Cormac Price/Shutterstock, 127 (bottom), 171 (top); cinoby/E+/Getty Images, 128; imageBROKER/Anette Mossbacher/Getty Images, 129; Heyfetz Eduard/Shutterstock, 130; R. Andrew Odum/Photodisc/Getty Images, 131; Agus_Gatam/Shutterstock, 132 (top); phalder/iStock/Getty Images, 132 (middle); Scott Delony/Shutterstock, 133 (top left); Chantelle Bosch/Shutterstock, 133 (top right); David Northcott/Danita Delimont Photography/Newscom, 133 (bottom); Tim_Booth/Shutterstock, 134; Natalia Golovina/Shutterstock, 135; Richard Susanto/Shutterstock, 136–137; Sergey Uryadnikov/Shutterstock, 138; Paul Souders/Stone/Getty Images, 139; Shahzad Siddiqui/Moment/Getty Images, 140; annick vanderschelden photography/Moment/Getty Images, 142; Tomas Drahos/Shutterstock, 143; Manoj Shah/Photodisc/Getty Images, 144; Ruzhdi Ibrahimi/500px/Getty Images, 146; Karel Bartik/Shutterstock, 147 (top); James Hager/robertharding/Collection Mix: Subjects/Getty Images, 147 (bottom); Fanie Heymans/500px/Getty Images, 148; Tara N Salgado/Shutterstock, 149; Bob Krist/The Image Bank/Getty Images, 150 (top); Andy119/Shutterstock, 150 (bottom); Martin Pelanek/Shutterstock, 151; George D. Lepp/Corbis Documentary/Getty Images, 152; Gerard Soury/The Image Bank/Getty Images, 153 (top); Johan Swanepoel/Shutterstock, 153 (bottom); Zhanna Muzalevskaia/iStock/Getty Images, 156 (top); Kathy Kay/Shutterstock, 156 (middle); digital fly/Moment/Getty Images, 156 (bottom); Aivaras Grauzinis/500px/Getty Images, 157 (top left); Michael Potter11/Shutterstock, 157 (top right); Nilanka Sampath/Shutterstock, 157 (bottom); Fiona Ayerst/Shutterstock, 158–159; lorenza62/Shutterstock, 159; tane-mahuta/iStock/Getty Images, 160; feathercollector/Shutterstock, 161 (top); Mark Chivers/Moment/Getty Images, 162; Grigorev Mikhail/Shutterstock, 163 (top); User10095428_393/iStock/Getty Images, 163 (bottom); by wildestanimal/Moment/Getty Images, 164; Pavaphon Supanantananont/Shutterstock, 165; crisod/iStock/Getty Images, 166 (middle); LuismiX/Moment/Getty Images, 167 (top); Fotokon/Shutterstock, 167 (middle); Denja1/iStock/Getty Images, 167 (bottom); Stu Porter/Shutterstock, 168; simplydave/iStock/Getty Images, 169; Holly Mahaffey Photography/Moment/Getty Images, 170; xpixel/Shutterstock, 171 (bottom); meunierd/Shutterstock, 172; Andre Coetzer/Shutterstock, 174; Dani Jara/Shutterstock, 175 (top); SteveAllenPhoto/iStock/Getty Images, 175 (bottom); reptiles4all/iStock/Getty Images, 176 (top); Paul Starosta/Stone/Getty Images, 176 (middle); davemhuntphotography/iStock/Getty Images, 176 (bottom); 25ehaag6/iStock/Getty Images, 177 (top); Sandberger-Loua L, Müller H, Rödel M-O/Wikimedia Commons, 177 (middle); Hurly D'souza/Shutterstock, 177 (bottom); Lucian Coman/Shutterstock, 178; Paulrommer SL/Shutterstock, 179 (left); Milan Zygmunt/Shutterstock, 179 (right); Jacqueline Brummans/500px/500Px Plus/Getty Images, 180; Eckart Mayer/500px/Getty Images, 181 (top); Gallo Images/Brand X Pictures/Getty Images, 181 (bottom); Audrey Snider-Bell/Shutterstock, 182 (top); Tomasz Kadelski/Dreamstime, 182 (bottom); ArtMediaFactory/Shutterstock, 183; macro_owadziarnia/500px/Getty Images, 184 (bottom); Pedro Bernardo/Shutterstock, 185 (top); Dr Morley Read/Shutterstock, 185 (bottom); cribea/iStock/Getty Images, 186 (top); KASIRA SUDA/Shutterstock, 186 (middle); Jeff Kingma/iStock/Getty Images, 186 (bottom); Olga Batalova/Shutterstock, 187 (top); Wipfler B, Theska T, Predel R (2018) Mantophasmatodea from the Richtersveld in South Africa with description of two new genera and species. ZooKeys 746: 137-160./Wikimedia Commons, 187 (middle); Thomas Quack/Shutterstock, 187 (bottom)

ABDOBOOKS.COM

Printed in China
052025
092025

Editor: Jane Katirgis
Series Designer: Colleen McLaren

LIBRARY OF CONGRESS CONTROL NUMBER: 2024949002

PUBLISHER'S CATALOGING-IN-PUBLICATION DATA

Names: Scott Royce, Brenda, author.
Title: The African animal encyclopedia / by Brenda Scott Royce
Description: Minneapolis, Minnesota : Abdo Reference, 2026 | Series: Animal encyclopedias | Includes online resources and index.
Identifiers: ISBN 9781098296575 (lib. bdg.) | ISBN 9798384918004 (ebook)
Subjects: LCSH: Zoology--Africa--Juvenile literature. | Animals--Juvenile literature. | Animals--Behavior--Juvenile literature. | Animal habitats--Juvenile literature. | Reference materials--Juvenile literature. | Encyclopedias and dictionaries--Juvenile literature.
Classification: DDC 590.3--dc23